babelcom

Hot! Spanish
for guys & girls

by David Appell
and Paul Balido

Other *Hot!* Titles

Second Edition
Copyright ©1995 by **BabelCom, Inc.**
231 West 16th Street, Suite 20
New York City, New York 10011 USA
800 468 9673 & 212 627 2074 *(phone)*
212 627 5209 *(fax)*
BABELCOM@AOL.COM *(e-mail)*
WWW.BABELCOM.COM *(Internet)*

ISBN 1-885948-22-0
Library of Congress Catalog Card Number: 95-76655

Manufactured in the United States of America

10   9   8   7   6   5   4   3

What's in the Book

APPENDIX

ForeWords

To be a traveler—not just a *turista*—means a lot more than whipping off snapshots of churches and statues. You've got to get down with the locals, and let's face it: It's educational, it's (usually) free, and it's fun! If you can talk, you can open doors—sometimes to a new understanding of their culture—sometimes even to their homes. Isn't this what travel is all about? Making new friends? Maybe a little romance? Or some great adventure you'll never forget?

Truth is, most people *love* tourists. They're sexy. They talk funny. They come from exotic places, like Idaho. You may never have thought of this, but *you* as a traveler—even in places used to cameras and burger joints—have a certain allure. Cash in on it! With the right attitude and a smattering of the language you could have far more fun in Madrid than Minneapolis.

And that's where the *Hot!* books come in. Other phrasebooks suggest you ask, "Do you play cards?" Or, if you really want to get down and funky, "Please play a foxtrot." We take up where they leave off—and then some. *Hot! Spanish* will get you through everything from friendly party chitchat to dating to steamy action in the sack. Plus what to say in the morning, and more.

Hot! Spanish could even be good for your health. A few key words can prevent crossed wires and keep you away from situations unsafe or unwanted. Awareness of AIDS and other diseases can vary quite a bit from country to country and person to person. Your new friend might be willing to jump right in unprotected, but you shouldn't be—and you should tell him or her as much.

A couple of general notes: Spanish, like many other languages, has two words for "you," one formal, one casual. These days most younger people use the informal *tú* instead of the formal *usted,* and so do we. Also, the terms in this book will be understood throughout Spain and Latin America, but when it comes to juicy stuff like body parts and doing the nasty, every country naturally has its own slang (*chingar,* for example, means "to fuck" in Mexico but not Spain). We'll point these out. And to keep things clear, we use the same words (*polla,* for example, for "cock") throughout, even though others are just as valid. You can find these variations in the *Hot! WordList* at the end of the book.

So, enough foreplay. *¡Buen viaje—y que te diviertas!* ("Have a good trip and a great time!")

FOREWORDS

Using the Book

USING THE BOOK

*H*ot! **Spanish** is easy! Before you know it, you could be chattering away—and maybe more. Just look in *What's in the Book*, find the section you need, turn to the right page, and you're ready to go! Here are a few notes to help you on your way:

All the phrases (except in the Appendix) have three forms: first the English, then the Spanish, and below that a phonetic version that you can pronounce more or less as if you're reading in English. The syllables in capital letters are the ones that get stressed. (You can double-check phonetic sounds like "dh" or "rroh" by looking them up in *Making the Sounds*, beginning on the next page.)

Words in parentheses are optional and can be left out of the sentence if you want. You can say *"(Muchas) gracias"*—"Thank you (very much)" or just *"Gracias"*—"Thank you." In the *Hot! WordList* at the end of the book, we also put feminine forms of masculine adjectives in parentheses. When you see *excitado (/-a)* under "aroused," this means that *excitado* turns into *excitada* for a woman.

Brackets ([ ]) are used in several different situations where there's a choice of words:

> When nouns or adjectives have male and female variants: "I'm crazy about you" is *"Estoy [loco / loca] por ti"* (a guy talking would say *loco* and a girl would say *loca*).

> When there are two possibilities in English for the same Spanish word: "I [want / desire] you" is *"Te deseo"* and "I love your [navel / belly button]" is *"Me encanta tu ombligo."*

> When we give you a choice of words to insert in the sentence: "Do you have a [boyfriend / girlfriend]?" is *"Tienes [novio / novia]?"*

When there are more than two or three choices in a sentence, they are listed in a box. "You're (very) ... ." can be combined with 27 different possibilities starting on page 74 to say "You're (very) sweet," "You're (very) sexy," and so forth.

If you don't already have any background in the language, definitely check out *A Fast 'n' Dirty Guide to Spanish,* starting on page 116, just to get a feel for how it all works.

That's it. Time for some *Hot!* Spanish!

MAKING THE SOUNDS

The sounds of Spanish are straightforward and regular (unlike in English, "a" is *always* "ah" and "u" is always "oo"). So once you get the hang of it, you won't even have to look at our pronunciation guides. For now, here's the Spanish alphabet:

Letter	Sound	Notes & Examples
b	b	softer than in English; *bailar* (to dance) is "bah-ee-LAHR"
c	th*	as in "thin" before "e" and "i"; *cita* (date) is "THEE-tah"
	k	as in English, but without the little puff of air, before "a," "o" and "u"; it's the "c" in "scone," not "cup"; *culo* (ass) is "KOO-loh"
ch	ch	as in English; *chocho* (cunt) is "CHOH-choh"
d	d	as in English at the beginning of a word or after "l" or "n"; *discoteca* (disco) is "deess-koh-TEH-kah"
	dh**	like "th" in "the" between vowels or after consonants other than "l" or "n"; *mamada* (blowjob) is "mah-MAH-dhah"
f	f	as in English; *falo* (phallus) is "FAH-loh"
g	g	as in "goat" (but softer) before "a," "o" and "u"; *garganta* (throat) is "gahr-GAHN-tah"
	h	as in "hotel" (but guttural—think of "Bach" or "loch") before "e" and "i"; *vagina* (vagina) is "vah-HEE-nah"
gu	gh	as in "guitar," but only before "e" and "i"; *alguien* (someone) is "AHL-ghee-ehn"
h	—	always silent; *hotel* (hotel) is "oh-TEHL"
j	h	as in "hotel" (but guttural—think of "Bach" or "loch"); *maja* (nice) is "MAH-hah"
k	k	as in English, but without the little puff of air; it's the "k" in "skate," not "king"; found mostly in foreign words; *kilómetro* (kilometer) is "kee-LOH-meh-troh"
l	l	as in English; *lamer* (to lick) is "lah-MEHR"

* "c" is like "th" only in Spain; if it's easier, say it like the Latin Americans—as an "s."
** If it's hard to nail down "d" *vs.* "dh," don't worry; say both like "d" and you're safe!

ForeWords

Making the Sounds

Letter	Sound	Notes & Examples
ll	y	technically like "lli" in "million," but most people pronounce it like a simple "y"; *follar* (to fuck) is "foh-YAHR"
m	m	as in English; *amor* (love) is "ah-MOHR"
n	n	as in English; *nalgas* (buttocks) is "NAHL-gahss"
ñ	ny	as in "canyon"—"n" and "y" combined; *cariño* (love, affection) is "kah-REE-nyoh"
p	p	as in English, but without the little puff of air: it's the "p" in "spin," not "Pop"; *pene* (penis) is "PEH-neh"
q	k	like "k" in English, but without the little puff of air; it's the "k" in "skate," not "king"; always followed by a silent "u"; *querer* (to love or want) is "keh-REHR"
r	r	a single flap of the tongue, the sound exists in American English as the "dd" in "shu*dd*er"; it never occurs at the beginning of a word; *cara* (face) is "KAH-rah"
[r / rr]	rr	a few rapid tongue flaps, like a kid making airplane sounds. If you just can't, you'll be understood if you say both "r" and "rr" as in English; *guarro* (sleazy) is "GWAH-rroh." At the beginning of a word, a single "r" is always doubled: *rabo* (cock) is "RRAH-boh"
s	s	as in English, but sharper in Spain, almost a hiss; *soso* (dull) is "SOH-soh"
	ss	same as a single "s," but at the end of a syllable we double up the "s" so you won't be tempted to pronounce it like the "s" in "Rose"
t	t	as in English, but without the little puff of air; it's the "t" in "stone," not "tank"; *tetas* (tits) is "TEH-tahss"
v	v	as in "Victor" but softer; *viejo verde* (dirty old man) is "vee-EH-hoh VEHR-dheh"
w	v	as in "Victor" but softer; rare in Spanish; *wáter* (toilet) is "VAH-tehr"
x	ks	as in English but not common; *excitante* (exciting) is "ehks-thee-TAHN-teh"
z	th*	as in "thin"; *hazlo* (do it) is "AHTH-loh"

* "z" is like "th" only in Spain; if it's easier, say it like the Latin Americans—as an "s."

Making the Sounds

Vowel(s)	Sound	Notes & Examples
a	ah	as in "father"; *alto* (tall) is "AHL-toh"
e	eh	as in "bed"; *ella* (she) is "EH-yah"
i	ee	as in "free"; *tipo* (guy) is "TEE-poh"
o	oh	similar to "oh" in English, but shorter, without the little "oo" sound at the end; *odio* (hate) is "OH-dhee-oh"
u	oo	as in English, but shorter; *chupar* (to suck) is "choo-PAHR"
ua	wah	like "wo" in "wonton"; *guarro* (sleazy) is "GWAH-rroh"
ue or üe	weh	like "we" in "wet"; *bueno* (good) is "BWEH-noh"; after "g," *ue* is pronounced "eh"
ui or üi	wee	as in English; *cuídate* (take care) is "KWEE-dhah-teh"; after "g," *ui* is pronounced "ee"
uo	woh	similar to "wa" in "wall"; *promiscuo* (promiscuous) is "proh-MEESS-kwoh"
y	y	as in English at the beginning of a syllable; *yo* (I) is "yoh"
	ee	as in "free" in diphthongs (vowel combinations) and by itself; *y* (and) is "ee"

Other vowel combinations are marked as separate sounds for clarity, but you should say them smoothly and quickly together as one syllable. For example, *hoy* (today) is pronounced "OH-ee" and *Uruguay* is "oo-roo-GWAH-ee."

Remember: Spanish vowels are short and pure, never long or drawled out as they often are in English. Also, some borrowed words are often pronounced pretty much like they are in English: el sex appeal, sexy, el S and M, topless.

STRESS

We show stressed syllables with capital letters: *crápula* (debauched) is pronounced "CRAH-poo-lah," not "crah-POO-lah." As a general note, Spanish words are stressed on the second-to-last syllable if the word ends in a vowel, "n" or "s;" or on the last syllable if it ends in a "y" or any consonant except "n" or "s." Exceptions are marked with a written accent mark (´) over the vowel, as in *crápula*.

¿ and ¡

These upside-down question and exclamation marks are used in writing in Spanish, but don't affect pronunciation.

AIDS UPDATE

Sex can be fun and fulfilling—but you don't want to get sick. And you certainly don't want to die. So when you do it, do it smart. It's not hard to avoid transmission of HIV and other nasty viruses if you follow some simple guidelines:

♥ ASSUME *everyone* is potentially infected, no matter how cute or sexy, and act accordingly. You can't tell someone's HIV status by his or her face or bod.

♥ SAFE & HOT: Cuddling, nibbling, masturbation, and rubbing bodies together. Deep kissing is OK except when you have open sores or cuts in your mouth, or if you've just brushed or flossed (your gums might bleed).

♥ FUCKING: Never do it "bareback"—without a condom—whether you're having vaginal or anal sex. To be extra safe, guys should pull out before coming. Condoms, though usually reliable, have been known to break.

♥ FELLATIO: Less risky than fucking, but if you want to be totally safe, just lick your partner's shaft; don't take the head in your mouth. Or you can use a condom (unlubricated is fine—and it'll taste better).

♥ CUNNILINGUS: Guys, for best protection put dental dams (little latex squares) or plastic wrap over her vagina or clitoris before going down on her. Or you can use a condom that you've cut open lengthwise.

♥ RIMMING (MOUTH TO ANUS): Generally considered a low risk for AIDS but a high risk for hepatitis and parasites. Use the same precautions you would for cunnilingus, above.

♥ TOYS: Dildos and vibrators are fine, but don't share them (or if you do, clean them carefully with bleach or rubbing alcohol and put a condom on them).

♥ RUBBER RULES: Make sure your condoms are latex—not lambskin or other animal skins. Also, never tear at condom packets with your teeth—you could tear the rubber!

♥ GREASE IT UP: If you need lubricant, make sure your brand is water-soluble (*not* oil- or fat-based, like baby oil, hand lotion, Crisco®, butter or Vaseline®!). The oil and fat break down the rubber. The best lubes contain nonoxynol-9, a spermicide—this may increase your protection—but *never* use a spermicide alone without an actual condom.

♥ DRINKING & DRUGS often do *not* mix with safer sex. You need your wits about you to keep it safe!

PERSONAL SAFETY

*Y*ou're more vulnerable in a foreign country than at home—especially if you travel alone. Keep important phone numbers handy, such as police, emergency rescue, and your embassy. Always carry identification with you, along with a contact name and number in your home country in case of emergency. And of course, let your family and/or friends know where you can be reached abroad.

Women especially: Get to know a guy before you venture off alone with him. If he's with friends, talk to them too. Get a sense of the guy. If *you're* with friends, make sure they—or at least a bartender—know you're leaving together and where you're going. If you're just not sure about him, think twice. If you're making a date with someone you don't know well, arrange to meet in public—not at his place.

Male or female, keep your wits about you. Promises of love have been sometimes used as setups for robbery or worse. And of course avoid dark streets, parks at night, and areas that looks unsafe. Your health and well-being *have to come first!*

¡ I M P O R T A N T !

You use *HOT! SPANISH FOR GUYS & GIRLS* AT YOUR OWN RISK. THE PHRASES IN THIS BOOK ARE MEANT TO HELP YOU COMMUNICATE WITH FRIENDS AND LOVERS SO THAT YOU CAN ENJOY YOURSELF *SAFELY* AND KEEP AWAY FROM DANGEROUS OR UNWANTED SITUATIONS. THE PUBLISHER DOES *NOT* UNDER ANY CIRCUMSTANCES ADVOCATE OR ENCOURAGE ANY ACTIVITIES THAT ARE HARMFUL TO YOUR HEALTH, SAFETY OR WELL-BEING. ANY DAMAGES, PHYSICAL OR OTHERWISE, THAT YOU CAUSE YOURSELF THROUGH YOUR OWN ACTIONS ARE *YOUR* RESPONSIBILITY AND THE PUBLISHER AND EDITORS CAN IN NO WAY ASSUME OR ACCEPT RESPONSIBILITY.

ABBREVIATIONS

adj.	adjective
adv.	adverb
arch.	archaic
Arg.	Argentine usage
D.R.	term used in the Dominican Republic
e.g.	for example
Eng.	English
equiv.	equivalent
fem.	feminine gender
fig.	figurative
gen.	general / generally
hum.	humorous / tongue-in-cheek
inf.	informal
L.A.	Latin American usage
lit.	literal / literally
masc.	masculine gender
med.	medical term
Mex.	Mexican usage
n.	noun
neg.	negative
phr.	phrase
pl.	plural
P.R.	Puerto Rican usage
pron.	pronounced
sing.	singular
s.o.	someone
Sp.	term used especially in Spain
spec.	specifically
usu.	usually
v.	verb

Basic Quickies

Yes.
Sí.
see.

Sure.
Claro.
KLAH-roh.

Maybe.
Quizá.
kee-THAH.

No.
No.
noh.

Please.
Por favor.
pohr fah-VOHR.

Thank you (very much).
(Muchas) gracias.
(MOO-chahss) GRAH-thee-ahss.

You're welcome.
De nada.
deh NAH-dhah.

Excuse me.
Perdón.
pehr-DOHN.

I'm sorry.
Lo siento.
loh see-EHN-toh.

Don't.
Para.
PAH-rah.

Not without a condom.
No sin condón.
noh seen kohn-DOHN.

Help!
¡Socorro!
soh-KOH-rroh!

FOR MORE BASICS, SEE APPENDIX A: *HANDY LITTLE WORDS* (P. 104).

Breaking the Ice

HI & BYE

Good [morning / day].
Buenos días.
BWEH-nohss DEE-ahss.

Good [afternoon / evening].
Buenas tardes.
BWEH-nahss TAHR-dehss.

[Hello / Hi].
Hola.
OH-lah.

Hello. *(on phone)*
Diga.
DEE-gah.

How're you doing?
¿Cómo estás?
KOH-moh ehss-TAHSS?

Fine, (thanks).
Muy bien, (gracias).
mwee bee-EHN, (GRAH-thee-ahss).

Not bad.
Tirando.
tee-RAHN-doh.

And you?
¿Y tú?
ee TOO?

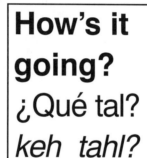

How's it going?
¿Qué tal?
keh tahl?

[Goodbye / Bye].
Adiós.
ah-dhee-OHSS.

See you later.
Hasta luego.
AHSS-tah LWEH-goh.

See you soon.
Hasta pronto.
AHSS-tah PROHN-toh.

Take care.
Cuídate.
KWEE-dhah-teh.

Good night.
Buenas noches.
BWEH-nahss NOH-chehss.

SAY WHAT?

(Sorry,) I don't understand.
(Lo siento,) no entiendo.
(loh see-EHN-toh,) noh ehn-tee-EHN-doh.

I don't speak Spanish (very well).
No hablo español (muy bien).
noh AH-bloh ehss-pah-NYOHL (mwee bee-EHN).

Do you speak English?
¿Hablas inglés?
AH-blahss een-GLEHSS?

(Please) slow down.
(Por favor) más despacio.
(pohr fa-VOHR,) mahss dehss-PAH-thee-oh.

What does ... mean?
¿Qué quiere decir ... ?
keh kee-EH-reh dheh-THEER ... ?

Do you have a dictionary?
¿Tienes diccionario?
tee-EH-nehss deek-thee-oh-NAH-ree-oh?

CLASSIC OPENINGS

Do you have the time?
¿Qué hora es?
keh OH-rah ehss?

SEE APPENDIX A: *CLOCKWISE* (P. 108).

Do you have a cigarette?
¿Tienes un cigarrillo?
tee-EH-nehss oon thee-gah-RREE-yoh?

Would you like a cigarette?
¿Quieres un cigarrillo?
kee-EH-rehss oon thee-gah-RREE-yoh?

Do you have a light?
¿Tienes fuego?
tee-EH-nehss FWEH-goh?

Here you go.
Toma.
TOH-mah.

Do you come here a lot?
¿Vienes mucho por aquí?
vee-EH-nehss MOO-choh pohr ah-KEE?

Don't I know you?
Me parece que te conozco.
meh pah-REH-theh keh teh koh-NOHTH-koh.

I've seen you [here / around] before.
Te he visto [aquí / por ahí] antes.
teh eh VEESS-toh [ah-KEE / pohr ah-EE] AHN-tehss.

You look so familiar.
Tu cara me suena.
too KAH-rah meh SWEH-nah.

Want some company?
¿Quieres que charlemos un rato?
kee-EH-rehss keh chahr-LEH-mohss oon RRAH-toh?

I like your [perfume / cologne].
Me gusta tu [perfume / colonia].
meh GOOSS-tah too [pehr-FOO-meh / koh-LOH-nee-ah].

What [perfume / cologne] are you wearing?
¿Qué [perfume / colonia] llevas?
keh [pehr-FOO-meh / koh-LOH-nee-ah] YEH-vahss?

¡ H E L P F U L   H I N T !

Y ou'll get a lot further if you keep it cool. Some of the phrases in this book are great to know, but you wouldn't always want to try them on a first meeting—or even a first date. Especially in more conservative parts of the world, too strong a come-on can sometimes be a turn-off for guys and girls alike (even if you *are* a tourist!).

Chit & Chat

BARS & DARK PLACES

This is a great [bar / disco].
Está muy bien [este bar / esta discoteca].
ehss-TAH mwee bee-EHN [EHSS-teh bahr / EHSS-tah dheess-koh-TEH-kah].

Good music, (huh?)
La música está bien, (¿eh?)
lah MOO-see-kah ehss-TAH bee-EHN, (eh?)

The [video / show] is great.
Ese [vídeo / espectáculo] está muy bien.
EH-seh [VEE-dheh-oh / ehss-pek-TAH-koo-loh] ehss-TAH mwee bee-EHN.

This music's the pits.
Esta música es pésima.
EHSS-tah MOO-see-kah ehss PEH-see-mah.

The [video / show] is the pits.
Ese [vídeo / espectáculo] es pésimo.
EH-seh [VEE-dheh-oh / ehss-pehk-TAH-koo-loh] ehss PEH-see-moh.

You like this song?
¿Te gusta esta canción?
teh GOOSS-tah EHSS-tah kahn-thee-OHN?

I like this song.
Me gusta esta canción.
meh GOOSS-tah EHSS-tah kahn-thee-OHN.

What's the name of this song?
¿Cómo se llama esta canción?
KOH-moh seh YAH-mah EHSS-tah kahn-thee-OHN?

Who's singing?
¿Quién canta?
kee-EHN KAHN-tah?

What kind of music do you like?
¿Qué clase de música te gusta?
keh KLAH-seh dheh MOO-see-kah teh GOOSS-tah?

Bars & Dark Places ♥ Out & About

Want to dance?
¿Quieres bailar?
kee-EH-rehss bah-ee-LAHR?

You're a great dancer.
Bailas muy bien.
BAH-ee-lahss mwee bee-EHN.

I can't hear you (well).
No te oigo (bien).
noh teh OH-ee-goh (bee-EHN).

It's too ... here.
Hay ... aquí.
AH-ee ... ah-KEE.

loud	smoky	crowded
demasiado	demasiado	demasiada
ruido	humo	gente
dheh-mah-	*dheh-mah-*	*dheh-mah-*
see-AH-	*see-AH-*	*see-AH-*
dhoh rroo-	*dhoh*	*dhah*
EE-dhoh	*OO-moh*	*HEHN-teh*

It's too [cold / hot] here.
Hace demasiado [frío / calor] aquí.
AH-theh dheh-mah-see-AH-dhoh [FREE-oh / kah-LOHR] ah-KEE.

Let's go over there.
Vamos para allá.
VAH-mohss PAH-rah ah-YAH.

Where's the restroom?
¿Dónde está el baño?
DOHN-deh ehss-TAH ehl BAH-nyoh?

SEE APPENDIX A: *WHERE?* (P. 106).

OUT & ABOUT

Nice weather, (isn't it?)
Qué buen tiempo, (¿eh?)
keh bwehn tee-EHM-poh, (eh?)

Lousy weather, (isn't it?)
Qué mal tiempo, (¿eh?)
keh mahl tee-EHM-poh, (eh?)

I love [this / this place].
Me encanta [esto / este sitio].
meh ehn-KAHN-tah [EHSS-toh / EHSS-teh SEE-tee-oh].

I don't care for [this / this place].
No me gusta [esto / este sitio].
noh meh GOOSS-tah [EHSS-toh / EHSS-teh SEE-tee-oh].

Do you like it?
¿Te gusta a ti?
teh GOOSS-tah ah tee?

TO GIVE HER OR HIM A COMPLIMENT, SEE *MUTUAL ADMIRATION SOCIETY* (P. 74).

COCKTAILS FOR TWO

Let me buy you a drink.
Te invito a una copa.
teh een-VEE-toh ah OO-nah KOH-pah.

I'm not drinking, thank you.
No tomo nada, gracias.
noh TOH-moh NAH-dhah, GRAH-thee-ahss.

Cheers!
¡Salud!
sah-LOODH!

What'll you have?
¿Qué tomas?
keh TOH-mahss?

I'll have ... .
Tráeme ... .
TRAH-eh-meh ... .

---

a [beer / draft beer]
una [cerveza / caña]
OO-nah [ther-VEH-thah / KAH-nyah]

a [red / white] wine
un vino [tinto / blanco]
oon VEE-noh [TEEN-toh / BLAHN-koh]

a glass of champagne
una copa de champán
OO-nah KOH-pah dheh chahm-PAHN

some juice
un zumo
oon THOO-moh

(iced) tea
un té (frío)
oon teh (FREE-oh)

a coffee (with milk)
un café (con leche)
oon kah-FEH (kohn LEH-cheh)

a [sparkling / flat] mineral water
un agua mineral [con / sin] gas
oon AH-gwah mee-neh-RAHL [kohn / seen] gahss

a cola
una coca-cola
OO-nah KOH-kah KOH-lah

... with ice
... con hielo
... kohn YEH-loh

... with lemon
... con limón
... kohn lee-MOHN

SMOKESCREENS

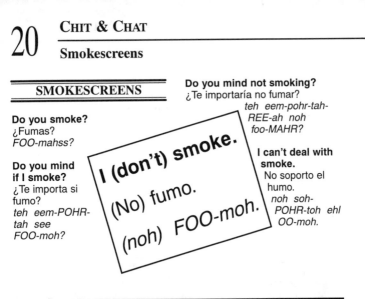

Do you smoke?
¿Fumas?
FOO-mahss?

Do you mind if I smoke?
¿Te importa si fumo?
teh eem-POHR-tah see FOO-moh?

I (don't) smoke.

(No) fumo.

(noh) FOO-moh.

Do you mind not smoking?
¿Te importaría no fumar?
teh eem-pohr-tah-REE-ah noh foo-MAHR?

I can't deal with smoke.
No soporto el humo.
noh soh-POHR-toh ehl OO-moh.

¡HELPFUL HINT!

For better or worse, you'll find Europeans and Latin Americans more easygoing than Americans about smoking. Our advice: When asking people not to smoke, be mellow and polite. It may or may not work, but an aggressive American approach could be met with ridicule—or worse. Best bet: If you can't stand the smoke, get out of the bar.

Introductions

DO-IT-YOURSELF

My name is ... .
Me llamo ... .
meh YAH-moh ... .

What's your name?
¿Cómo te llamas?
KOH-moh teh YAH-mahss?

Again, please?
¿Cómo?
KOH-moh?

Nice to meet you.
Mucho gusto.
MOO-choh GOOSS-toh.

Is this your [boyfriend / husband]?
¿Es tu [novio / marido]?
ehss too [NOH-vee-oh / mah-REE-dhoh]?

This is my [friend / ex].
Éste es mi [amigo / ex].
EHSS-teh ehss mee [ah-MEE-goh / ehks].

That (over there) is my [boyfriend / husband].
Aquél es mi [novio / marido].
ah-KEHL ehss mee [NOH-vee-oh / mah-REE-dhoh].

Is this your [girlfriend / wife]?
¿Es tu [novia / mujer]?
ehss too [NOH-vee-ah / moo-HEHR]?

This is my [friend / ex].
Ésta es mi [amiga / ex].
EHSS-tah ehss mee [ah-MEE-gah / ehks].

That (over there) is my [girlfriend / wife].
Aquélla es mi [novia / mujer].
ah-KEH-yah ehss mee [NOH-vee-ah / moo-HEHR].

What's [his / her] name?
¿Cómo se llama?
KOH-moh seh YAH-mah?

[His / Her] name is ... .
Se llama ... .
seh YAH-mah ... .

OUTSIDE HELP

Do you know ... ?
¿Conoces a ... ?
koh-NOH-thehss ah ... ?

that girl	that guy
aquella chica	aquel chico
ah-KEH-yah	*ah-KEHL*
CHEE-kah	*CHEE-koh*
that woman	that man
aquella mujer	aquel hombre
ah-KEH-yah	*ah-KEHL*
moo-HEHR	*OHM-breh*

I'd like to meet [her / him].
Me gustaría [conocerla / conocerlo].
meh gooss-tah-REE-ah [koh-noh-THEHR-lah / koh-noh-THEHR-loh].

Can you take [her / him] a drink?
¿Le llevas esta copa?
leh YEH-vahss EHSS-tah KOH-pah?

Tell [her / him] I like [her / him].
Dile que me gusta mucho.
DEE-leh keh meh GOOSS-tah MOO-choh.

Can you introduce us?
¿Nos puedes presentar?
nohss PWEH-dehss preh-sehn-TAHR?

This is ... .
Te presento a ... .
teh preh-SEHN-toh ah ... .

This is my [female / male] friend ... .
[Ésta es mi amiga / Éste es mi amigo] ... .
[EHSS-tah ehss mee ah-MEE-gah / EHSS-teh ehss mee ah-MEE-goh] ... .

These are my [female / male or mixed] friends ... and ... .
[Éstas son mis amigas / Éstos son mis amigos] ... y ... .
[EHSS-tahss sohn meess ah-MEE-gahss / EHSS-tohss sohn meess ah-MEE-gohss] ... ee ....

Digging Deeper

PLACES CALLED HOME

Where are you from?
¿De dónde eres?
deh DHOHN-deh EH-rehss?

I'm from ... .
Soy de ... .
SOH-ee dheh ... .

Are you from ... ?
¿Eres de ... ?
EH-rehss deh ... ?

the United States	Scotland	Australia
los Estados Unidos	Escocia	Australia
lohss ehss-TAH-dhohss	*ehss-KOH-thee-ah*	*ah-ooss-TRAH-lee-ah*
oo-NEE-dhohss		
		New Zealand
Canada	**Wales**	Nueva Zelanda
Canadá	Gales	*NWEH-vah theh-LAHN-*
kah-nah-DHAH	*GAH-lehss*	*dah*
England	**Ireland**	**South Africa**
Inglaterra	Irlanda	Suráfrica
een-glah-TEH-rrah	*eer-LAHN-dah*	*soor-AH-free-kah*

FOR OTHER COUNTRIES & NATIONALITIES, SEE APPENDIX C: *PEOPLE & PLACES* (P. 113).

I'm from [New York / Madrid].
Soy de [Nueva York / Madrid].
SOH-ee dheh [NWEH-vah yohrk
/ mah-DHREEDH].

But I live [in Mexico / here].
Pero vivo [en México / aquí].
PEH-roh VEE-voh [ehn
MEH-hee-koh / ah-KEE].

STAYING LONG?

How long are you staying?
¿Cuánto tiempo te vas a quedar?
*KWAHN-toh tee-EHM-poh teh
vahss ah keh-DHAHR?*

I'm leaving ... .
Me voy ... .
meh VOH-ee ... .

tomorrow mañana *mah-NYAH-nah*	in (three) [days / weeks / months] en (tres) [días / semanas/ meses]
the day after tomorrow pasado mañana *pah-SAH-dhoh mah-NYAH-nah*	*ehn (trehss) [DEE-ahss / seh-MAH-nahss / MEH-sehss].*

SEE ALSO APPENDIX A: *WHEN?* (P. 105),
AND *A ONE AND A TWO...* (P. 107).

COMING & GOING

What brings you here?
¿Qué haces aquí?
keh AH-thehss ah-KEE?

I'm on vacation.
Estoy de vacaciones.
*ehss-TOH-ee dheh
vah-kah-thee-OH-nehss.*

I'm studying here.
Estudio aquí.
ehss-TOO-dhee-oh ah-KEE.

I'm here on business.
Estoy de negocios.
*ehss-TOH-ee dheh
neh-GOH-thee-ohss.*

I live here.
Vivo aquí.
VEE-voh ah-KEE.

I'm visiting [friends / family].
He venido a ver a unos [amigos /
parientes].
*eh veh-NEE-dhoh ah vehr ah
OO-nohss [ah-MEE-gohss /
pah-ree-EHN-tehss].*

Welcome (to Spain).
[Bienvenido / Bienvenida]
(a España).
*[bee-ehn-veh-NEE-dhoh /
bee-ehn-veh-NEE-dhah
(ah ehss-PAH-nyah).*

How do you like it here?
¿Te gusta esto?
teh GOOSS-tah EHSS-toh?

I like it a lot.
Me encanta.
meh ehn-KAHN-tah.

THE STUDENT BODY

Where do you study?
¿Dónde estudias?
DOHN-deh ehss-TOO-dhee-ahss?

What do you study?
¿Qué estudias?
keh ehss-TOO-dhee-ahss?

I'm studying ... .
Estudio ... .
ehss-TOO-dhee-oh ... .

accounting
contabilidad
kohn-tah-bee-lee-DHADH

acting
teatro
teh-AH-troh

architecture
arquitectura
ahr-kee-tehk-TOO-rah

art
arte
AHR-teh

business
ciencias empresariales
*thee-EHN-thee-ahss
ehm-preh-sah-ree-
AH-lehss*

computer science
informática
een-fohr-MAH-tee-kah

economics
economía
eh-koh-noh-MEE-ah

engineering
ingeniería
een-heh-nyeh-REE-ah

English
inglés
een-GLEHSS

history
historia
eess-TOH-ree-ah

**hotel and restaurant
management**
hostelería
ohss-teh-leh-REE-ah

journalism
periodismo
peh-ree-oh-DHEESS-moh

languages
idiomas
ee-dhee-OH-mahss

law
derecho
dheh-REH-choh

literature
literatura
lee-teh-rah-TOO-rah

medicine
medicina
meh-dhee-THEE-nah

music
música
MOO-see-kah

philosophy
filosofía
fee-loh-soh-FEE-ah

political science
ciencias políticas
*thee-EHN-thee-ahss
poh-LEE-tee-kahss*

psychology
psicología
see-koh-loh-HEE-ah

science
ciencias
thee-EHN-thee-ahss

GET A JOB

What do you do for a living?
¿En qué trabajas?
ehn keh trah-BAH-hahss?

BOTH MALE & FEMALE FORMS ARE GIVEN IN THE TABLE BELOW WHERE APPROPRIATE.

I have my own business.
Tengo mi propio negocio.
TEHN-goh mee PROH-pee-oh neh-GOH-thee-oh.

I'm ... .
Yo ... .
yoh ... .

---

an accountant
soy contable
SOH-ee kohn-TAH-bleh

an [actor / actress]
soy [actor / actriz]
SOH-ee [ahk-TOHR / ahk-TREETH]

in advertising
trabajo en una agencia publicitaria
trah-BAH-hoh ehn OO-nah ah-HEHN-thee-ah poo-blee-thee-TAH-ree-ah

an artist
soy artista
SOH-ee ahr-TEESS-tah

an athlete
soy atleta
SOH-ee aht-LEH-tah

in banking
trabajo en un banco
trah-BAH-hoh ehn oon BAHN-koh

a bartender
soy [camarero / camarera] (de bar)
SOH-ee [kah-mah-REH-roh / kah-mah-REH-rah] (dheh bahr)

a [businessman / businesswoman]
soy [hombre / mujer] de negocios
SOH-ee [OHM-breh / moo-HEHR] dheh neh-GOH-thee-ohss

a dancer
soy [bailarín / bailarina]
SOH-ee [bah-ee-lah-REEN / bah-ee-lah-REE-nah]

a designer
soy [diseñador / diseñadora]
SOH-ee [dhee-seh-nyah-DHOHR / dhee-seh-nyah-DHOH-rah]

a director
soy [director / directora]
SOH-ee [dhee-rehk-TOHR / dhee-rehk-TOH-rah]

a doctor
soy [médico / médica]
SOH-ee [MEH-dhee-koh / MEH-dhee-kah]

an editor
soy [redactor / redactora]
SOH-ee [rreh-dhahk-TOHR / rreh-dhahk-TOH-rah]

a flight attendant
soy asistente de vuelo
SOH-ee ah-seess-TEHN-teh dheh VWEH-loh

a journalist
soy periodista
SOH-ee peh-ree-oh-DHEESS-tah

a lawyer
soy [abogado / abogada]
SOH-ee [ah-boh-GAH-dhoh / ah-boh-GAH-dhah]

doing military service
estoy en la mili
ehss-TOH-ee ehn lah MEE-lee

[COMPULSORY IN MANY COUNTRIES]

in the military
soy militar
SOH-ee mee-lee-TAHR

a model
soy modelo
SOH-ee moh-DHEH-loh

a musician
soy músico
SOH-ee MOO-see-koh

a nurse
soy [enfermero / enfermera]
SOH-ee [ehn-fehr-MEH-roh / ehn-fehr-MEH-rah]

a photographer
soy [fotógrafo / fotógrafa]
SOH-ee [foh-TOH-grah-foh / foh-TOH-grah-fah]

a (university) professor
soy [profesor / profesora] (de universidad)
SOH-ee [proh-feh-SOHR / proh-feh-SOH-rah] (dheh oo-nee-vehr-see-DHADH)

a sales clerk
soy [dependiente / dependienta]
SOH-ee [dheh-pehn-dee-EHN-teh / dheh-pehn-dee-EHN-tah]

a sales- [man / woman]
soy representante de ventas
SOH-ee rreh-preh-sen-TAHN-teh dheh VEHN-tahss

a secretary
soy [secretario / secretaria]
SOH-ee [seh-kreh-TAH-ree-oh / seh-kreh-TAH-ree-ah]

a teacher
soy [maestro / maestra]
SOH-ee [mah-EHSS-troh / mah-EHSS-trah]

a travel agent
soy agente de viajes
SOH-ee ah-HEHN-teh dheh vee-AH-hehss

unemployed
estoy en paro
ehss-TOH-ee ehn PAH-roh

a waiter
soy [camarero / camarera]
SOH-ee [kah-mah-REH-roh / kah-mah-REH-rah]

a writer
soy [escritor / escritora]
SOH-ee [ehss-kree-TOHR / ehss-kree-TOH-rah]

THE YOUNG AND THE OLDER

How old are you?
¿Cuántos años tienes?
KWAHN-tohss AH-nyohss tee-EH-nehss?

I'm [twenty-five / thirty-two] years old.
Tengo [veinticinco / treinta y dos] años.
TEHN-goh [veh-een-tee-THEEN-koh / TREH-een-tah ee dhohss] AH-nyohss.

FOR MORE NUMBERS, SEE APPENDIX A: *A ONE AND A TWO...* (P. 107).

You look very young.
Pareces muy joven.
pah-REH-thehss mwee HOH-vehn.

You look [younger / older].
Pareces [más joven / mayor].
pah-REH-thehss [mahss HOH-vehn / mah-YOHR].

STARSTRUCK

What's your sign?
¿De qué signo eres?
deh keh SEEG-noh EH-rehss?

I'm ... .
Soy ... .
SOH-ee ... .

Aquarius acuario *ah-KWAH-ree-oh*	**Libra** libra *LEE-brah*
Aries aries *AH-ree-ehss*	**Pisces** piscis *PEESS-theess*
Cancer cáncer *KAHN-thehr*	**Sagittarius** sagitario *sah-hee-TAH-ree-oh*
Capricorn capricornio *kah-pree-KOHR-nee-oh*	**Scorpio** escorpión *ehss-kohr-pee-OHN*
Gemini géminis *HEH-mee-neess*	**Taurus** tauro *TAH-oo-roh*
Leo leo *LEH-oh*	**Virgo** Virgo *VEER-goh*

ATTACHED?
(& HOW MUCH)

Are you seeing someone?
¿Sales con alguien?
SAH-lehss kohn AHL-ghee-ehn?

I'm seeing someone.
Salgo con alguien.
SAHL-goh kohn AHL-ghee-ehn.

I'm not seeing anyone.
No salgo con nadie.
noh SAHL-goh kohn NAH-dhee-eh.

I'm (not) single.
(No) estoy [soltero / soltera].
(noh) ehss-TOH-ee [sohl-TEH-roh / sohl-TEH-rah].

Do you have a [boyfriend / girlfriend]?
¿Tienes [novio / novia]?
tee-EH-nehss [NOH-vee-oh / NOH-vee-ah]?

Are you single?
¿Estás [soltero / soltera]?
ehss-TAHSS [sohl-TEH-roh / sohl-TEH-rah]?

I (don't) have a [boyfriend / girlfriend].
(No) tengo [novio / novia].
(noh) TEHN-goh [NOH-vee-oh / NOH-vee-ah].

We have an open relationship.
Tenemos una relación abierta.
Teh-NEH-mohss OO-nah rreh-lah-thee-OHN ah-bee-EHR-tah.

I'm [gay / lesbian].
Soy [homosexual / lesbiana].
SOH-ee [oh-moh-sehk-SWAHL / lehss-bee-AH-nah].

IN SPANISH-SPEAKING COUNTRIES, HETEROSEX-UALS USUALLY REFER TO GAYS AS *HOMOSEXUAL*, WHILE HOMOSEXUALS OFTEN CALL THEMSELVES *GAY* OR *LESBIANA*.

I'm engaged.
Estoy [prometido / prometida].
ehss-TOH-ee [proh-meh-TEE-dhoh / proh-meh-TEE-dhah].

That's too bad.
Qué lástima.
keh LAHSS-tee-mah.

DIGGING DEEPER

Attached? (& How Much)

I'd still like to get to know you.
Aún así quisiera conocerte.
*ah-OON ah-SEE kee-see-EH-rah
koh-noh-THEHR-teh.*

Are you married?
Estás [casado / casada]?
*ehss-TAHSS [kah-SAH-dhoh /
kah-SAH-dhah]?*

I'm (not) married.
(No) estoy [casado / casada].
*(noh) ehss-TOH-ee [kah-SAH-
dhoh / kah-SAH-dhah].*

I have an open marriage.
Tengo un matrimonio abierto.
*TEHN-goh oon mah-tree-MOH-
nee-oh ah-bee-EHR-toh.*

**I'm separated from my
husband.**
Estoy separada de mi marido.
*ehss-TOH-ee seh-pah-RAH-dhah
dheh mee mah-REE-dhoh.*

I'm separated from my wife.
Estoy separado de mi mujer.
*ehss-TOH-ee seh-pah-RAH-dhoh
dheh mee moo-HEHR.*

I'm divorced.
Estoy [divorciado / divorciada].
*ehss-TOH-ee [dhee-vohr-thee-
AH-dhoh / dhee-vohr-thee-
AH-dhah].*

I'm getting a divorce.
Estoy en proceso de divorciarme.
*ehss-TOH-ee ehn proh-THEH-
soh dheh dhee-vohr-thee-
AHR-meh.*

I'm widowed.
Soy [viudo / viuda].
*SOH-ee [vee-OO-dhoh /
vee-OO-dhah].*

I'm so sorry.
Lo siento muchísimo.
*loh see-EHN-toh moo-CHEE-
see-moh.*

Do you have children?
¿Tienes hijos?
tee-EH-nehss EE-hohss?

Two daughters and a son.
Dos hijas y un hijo.
*dohss EE-hahss ee oon
EE-hoh.*

FOR OTHER NUMBERS, SEE APPENDIX A:
A ONE AND A TWO... (P. 107).

Popping the Question

THE DIRECT APPROACH

I like you a lot.
Me caes muy bien.
meh KAH-ehss mwee bee-EHN.

SEE ALSO *MUTUAL ADMIRATION SOCIETY* (P. 74).

I want to go to bed with you.
Quiero acostarme contigo.
kee-EH-roh ah-kohss-TAHR-meh kohn-TEE-goh.

Let's get to know each other better first.
Vamos a esperar a conocernos mejor.
VAH-mohss ah ehss-peh-RAHR ah koh-noh-THEHR-nohss meh-HOHR.

SEE ALSO *SURE THING!* (P. 33), *SEE YOU LATER* (P. 34), *NO, THANKS* (P. 35), & *GO AWAY!* (P. 36).

MAKING AN OFFER

Want to go somewhere?
¿Vamos a alguna parte?
VAH-mohss ah ahl-GOO-nah PAHR-teh?

Want to go for ... ?
¿Quieres ... ?
kee-EH-rehss ... ?

a walk	coffee
dar un paseo	tomar un café
dahr oon	*toh-MAHR oon*
pah-SEH-oh	*kah-FEH*
something to eat	a drink
comer algo	tomar una copa
koh-MEHR	*toh-MAHR*
AHL-goh	*OO-nah*
	KOH-pah

Want to get out of here?
¿Salimos?
sah-LEE-mohss?

Where can we go?
¿Adónde vamos?
ah-DHOHN-deh VAH-mohss?

Making an Offer ♥ My Place or Yours

I know a place.
Conozco un sitio.
*koh-NOHTH-koh oon
SEE-tee-oh.*

Let's go somewhere else.
Vamos a otro sitio.
*VAH-mohss ah OH-troh
SEE-tee-oh.*

Over there.
Allá.
ah-YAH.

Not here.
Aquí no.
ah-KEE noh.

People can see us.
Nos pueden ver.
nohss PWEH-dehn vehr.

Want to come home for a drink?
¿Vamos a casa a tomar una copa?
VAH-mohss ah KAH-sah ah toh-MAHR OO-nah KOH-pah?

Want to go to [my place / your place]?
¿Vamos a [mi / tu] casa?
VAH-mohss ah [mee / too] KAH-sah?

MY PLACE OR YOURS

Where are you staying?
¿Dónde te quedas?
DOHN-deh teh KEH-dhahss?

I'm at the _____ Hotel.
Estoy en el hotel _____ .
ehss-TOH-ee ehn ehl oh-TEHL _____ .

Do you live by yourself?
¿Vives [solo / sola]?
VEE-vehss [SOH-loh / SOH-lah]?

I live alone.
Vivo [solo / sola].
VEE-voh [SOH-loh / SOH-lah].

I live with my parents.
Vivo con mis padres.
VEE-voh kohn meess PAH-dhrehss.

I have a roommate.
Comparto piso.
kohm-PAHR-toh PEE-soh.

Is someone at home (now)?
¿Hay alguien en casa (ahora)?
AH-ee AHL-ghee-ehn ehn KAH-sah (ah-OH-rah)?

Sure Thing! (& Drunk Driving)

Someone's at home (tonight).
Hay alguien en casa (esta noche).
AH-ee AHL-ghee-ehn ehn KAH-sah (EHSS-tah NOH-cheh).

No one's at home (today).
No hay nadie en casa (hoy).
noh AH-ee NAH-dhee-eh ehn KAH-sah (OH-ee).

SURE THING!

I'd love to.
Me encantaría.
meh ehn-kahn-tah-REE-ah.

Let's go.
Vamos.
VAH-mohss.

I'll say goodbye to my ... .
Voy a despedirme de ... .
VOH-ee ah dhehss-peh-DHEER-meh dheh ... .

friend *(a guy)*	friend *(a girl)*
mi amigo	mi amiga
mee ah-MEE-goh	*mee ah-MEE-gah*
friends	**friends**
(guys / mixed)	*(girls only)*
mis amigos	mis amigas
meess ah-MEE-gohss	*meess ah-MEE-gahss*

I'll wait for you [here / over there].
Te espero [aquí / allí].
teh ehss-PEH-roh [ah-KEE / ah-YEE].

DRUNK DRIVING

[I'm / You're] drunk.
[He / Has] bebido demasiado.
[eh / ahss] beh-BEE-dhoh dheh-mah-see-AH-dhoh.

[I'm / You're] high.
[Me pasé / Te pasaste] con las drogas.
[meh pah-SEH / teh pah-SAHSS-teh] kohn lahss DROH-gahss.

We'd better not drive.
Mejor no conducir.
meh-HOHR noh kohn-doo-THEER.

Can *you* drive?
¿Puedes conducir *tú*?
PWEH-dhehss kohn-doo-THEER TOO?

I can drive.
Puedo conducir.
PWEH-dhoh kohn-doo-THEER.

Let's take a taxi.
Vamos a tomar un taxi.
VAH-mohss ah toh-MAHR oon TAHK-see.

SEE YOU LATER

Some other time.
Otro día.
OH-troh DHEE-ah

(I'm sorry,) I have to go.
(Lo siento,) me tengo que ir.
(loh see-EHN-toh,) meh TEHN-goh keh eer.

(But) I'd like to see you again.
(Pero) quisiera verte otra vez.
(PEH-roh) kee-see-EH-rah VEHR-teh OH-trah VEHTH.

Great to have met you.
Me alegro de haberte conocido.
meh ah-LEH-groh dheh ah-BEHR-teh koh-noh-THEE-dhoh.

It was nice talking to you.
Me encantó hablar contigo.
meh ehn-kahn-TOH ah-BLAHR kohn-TEE-goh.

I had a great time with you.
Lo he pasado muy bien contigo.
loh eh pah-SAH-dhoh mwee bee-EHN kohn-TEE-goh.

NAME & NUMBER

Can I have your phone number?
¿Me das tu número de teléfono?
meh dhahss too NOO-meh-roh dheh teh-LEH-foh-noh?

Do you have a business card?
¿Tienes una tarjeta de visita?
tee-EH-nehss OO-nah tahr-HEH-tah dheh vee-SEE-tah?

Here's my business card.
Toma mi tarjeta de visita.
TOH-mah mee tahr-HEH-tah dheh vee-SEE-tah.

Do you have a [pen / piece of paper]?
¿Tienes [lápiz / papel]?
tee-EH-nehss [LAH-peeth / pah-PEHL]?

Here's my phone number (and address).
Aquí tienes mi número de teléfono (y dirección).
ah-KEE tee-EH-nehss mee NOO-meh-roh dheh teh-LEH-foh-noh (ee dhee-rehk-thee-OHN).

Name & Number ♥ No, Thanks

This is my [hotel / home / work] number.
Éste es mi número [en el hotel / de casa / en el trabajo].
EHSS-teh ehss mee NOO-meh-roh [ehn ehl oh-TEHL / dheh KAH-sah / ehn ehl trah-BAH-hoh].

Call me at [my hotel / home / work].
Llámame [al hotel / en casa / al trabajo].
YAH-mah-me [ahl oh-TEHL / ehn KAH-sah / ahl trah-BAH-hoh].

Don't call me at my [hotel / home / work].
No me llames [al hotel / en casa / al trabajo].
noh meh YAH-mehss [ahl oh-TEHL / ehn KAH-sah / ahl trah-BAH-hoh].

I'll call you [tomorrow / soon / one of these days].
Te llamo [mañana / pronto / un día de éstos].
teh YAH-moh [mah-NYAH-nah / PROHN-toh / oon DEE-ah dheh EHSS-tohss].

I have an answering machine.
Tengo contestador.
TEHN-goh kohn-tehss-tah-DHOHR.

Be discreet.
Sé [discreto / discreta].
seh [dheess-KREH-toh / dheess-KREH-tah].

NO, THANKS

(I'd love to, but) I'm busy.
(Me encantaría, pero) estoy [ocupado / ocupada].
(meh ehn-kahn-tah-REE-ah, PEH-roh) ehss-TOH-ee [oh-koo-PAH-dhoh / oh-koo-PAH-dhah].

I have to go.
Tengo que irme.
TEHN-goh keh EER-meh.

I have to go find my ... .
Voy a buscar a ... .
VOH-ee ah booss-KAHR ah ...

friend *(a guy)*	friend *(a girl)*
mi amigo	mi amiga
mee ah-MEE-goh	*mee ah-MEE-gah*
friends *(guys / mixed)*	**friends** *(girls only)*
mis amigos	mis amigas
meess ah-MEE-gohss	*meess ah-MEE-gahss*

I'm in a hurry.
Tengo prisa.
TEHN-goh PREE-sah.

I'm (a little) tired.
Estoy (un poco) [cansado / cansada].
ehss-TOH-ee (oon POH-koh) [kahn-SAH-dhoh / kahn-SAH-dhah].

GO AWAY!

(Please) leave me alone.
(Por favor,) déjame en paz.
(pohr fah-VOHR) DEH-hah-meh ehn pahth.

Don't bother me.
No me molestes.
noh meh moh-LEHSS-tehss.

You're not my type.
No eres mi tipo.
noh EH-rehss mee TEE-poh.

I don't like you.
No me gustas.
noh meh GOOSS-tahss.

Get lost!
¡Lárgate!
LAHR-gah-teh!

Fuck off!
¡Vete a tomar por culo!
VEH-teh ah toh-MAHR pohr KOO-loh!

The Dating Game

PUTTING IT TOGETHER

I had a great time with you (tonight).
Lo pasé muy bien contigo (esta noche).
loh pah-SEH mwee bee-EHN kohn-TEE-goh (EHSS-tah NOH-cheh).

SEE ALSO APPENDIX A: *WHEN?* (P. 105).

I'd like to see you again.
Quisiera volverte a ver.
kee-see-EH-rah vohl-VEHR-teh ah vehr.

Me, too.
Yo también.
yoh tahm-bee-EHN.

Would you like to go ... ?
¿Te gustaría ir ... ?
teh gooss-tah-REE-ah eer ... ?

to dinner a cenar *ah theh-NAHR*	**to a party** a una fiesta *ah OO-nah fee-EHSS-tah*	**to a concert** a un concierto *ah oon kohn-thee-EHR-toh*	**to play tennis** a jugar al tenis *ah hoo-GAHR ahl TEH-neess*
for a drink a tomar una copa *ah toh-MAHR OO-nah KOH-pah*	**to a movie** al cine *ahl THEE-neh*	**to a museum** a un museo *ah oon moo-SEH-oh*	**[bicycling / for a drive]** a pasear en [bicicleta / coche] *ah pah-seh-AHR ehn [bee-thee-KLEH-tah / KOH-cheh]*
for ice cream a tomar un helado *ah toh-MAHR oon eh-LAH-dhoh*	**to the theater** al teatro *ahl teh-AH-troh*	**on a picnic** de picnic *dheh PEEK-neek*	**to my [house / hotel]** a mi [casa / hotel] *ah mee [KAH-sah / oh-TEHL]*
dancing a bailar *ah bah-ee-LAHR*	**to the opera** a la ópera *ah lah OH-peh-rah*	**to the beach** a la playa *ah lah PLAH-yah*	

Putting It Together ♥ Where & When

I'd like to cook dinner for you.
Me gustaría invitarte a cenar en casa.
meh gooss-tah-REE-ah een-vee-TAHR-teh ah theh-NAHR ehn KAH-sah.

TO RESPOND, SEE *SURE THING!* (P. 33) OR *NO, THANKS* (P. 35).

WHERE & WHEN

Are you busy ... ?
¿Estás [ocupado / ocupada] ... ?
ehss-TAHSS [oh-koo-PAH-dhoh / oh-koo-PAH-dhah] ... ?

Would you like to go out with me ... ?
¿Quisieras salir conmigo ... ?
kee-see-EH-rahss sah-LEER kohn-MEE-goh ... ?

today	[tomorrow / Friday] (night)
hoy	[mañana / el viernes] (por la noche)
OH-ee	
	[mah-NYAH-nah / ehl vee-EHR-nehss] (pohr lah NOH-cheh)
tonight	
esta noche	
EHSS-tah NOH-cheh	

SEE ALSO APPENDIX A: *IF IT'S TUESDAY...* (P. 109).

Let's meet at ... .
Vamos a encontrarnos en ... .
VAH-mohss ah ehn-kohn-TRAHR-nohss ehn ... .

[my / your] [place / hotel]	the movie theater
[mi / tu] [casa / hotel]	el cine
[mee / too] [KAH-sah / oh-TEHL]	*ehl THEE-neh*
the restaurant	**the theater**
el restaurante	el teatro
ehl rrehss-tah-oo-RAHN-teh	*ehl teh-AH-troh*
the bar	**the opera**
el bar	la ópera
ehl bahr	*lah OH-peh-rah*
the café	**the museum**
el café	el museo
ehl kah-FEH	*ehl moo-SEH-oh*
the ice cream parlor	**the beach**
la heladería	la playa
lah eh-lah-dheh-REE-ah	*lah PLAH-yah*
the disco	**the tennis court**
la discoteca	la cancha de tenis
lah dheess-koh-TEH-kah	*lah KAHN-chah dheh TEH-neess*
	the park
	el parque
	ehl PAHR-keh

Where & When ♥ Wining & Dining

Where is it?
¿Dónde queda?
DOHN-deh KEH-dhah?

Here's the address.
Toma la dirección.
TOH-mah lah dhee-rehk-thee-OHN.

It's at number _____, Republic Street.
Está en la calle República, número _____.
ehss-TAH ehn lah KAH-yeh rreh-POO-blee-kah, NOO-meh-roh _____.

FOR NUMBERS, SEE APPENDIX A: *A ONE AND A TWO...* (P. 107).

What time?
¿A qué hora?
ah keh OH-rah?

SEE APPENDIX A: *CLOCKWISE* (P. 108).

Don't be late.
No tardes.
noh TAHR-dhehss.

How should I dress?
¿Qué ropa me pongo?
keh RROH-pah meh POHN-goh?

Casual.	**Formal.**
Ropa informal.	De etiqueta.
RROH-pah een-fohr-MAHL.	*deh eh-tee-KEH-tah.*
Dress up.	**As you like.**
Arréglate bien.	Como quieras.
ah-RREH-glah-teh bee-EHN.	*KOH-moh kee-EH-rahss.*

It'll be my treat.
Te invito yo.
teh een-VEE-toh yoh.

WINING & DINING

Can you help me with the menu?
¿Me puedes ayudar con el menú?
meh PWEH-dhehss ah-yoo-DHAHR kohn ehl meh-NOO?

What would you like?
¿Qué quieres tomar?
keh kee-EH-rehss toh-MAHR?

I'm on a diet.
Estoy a dieta.
ehss-TOH-ee ah dhee-EH-tah.

I'm a vegetarian.
Soy [vegetariano / vegetariana].
SOH-ee [veh-heh-tah-ree-AH-noh / veh-heh-tah-ree-AH-nah].

What do you suggest?
¿Qué me recomiendas?
keh meh rreh-koh-mee-EHN-dahss?

I suggest [... / this].
Te recomiendo [... / esto].
teh rreh-koh-mee-EHN-doh [... / EHSS-toh].

Would you like ... ?
¿Quieres ... ?
kee-EH-rehss ... ?

I'd like ... .
Quisiera ... .
kee-see-EH-rah ... .

---

an apéritif
un aperitivo
oon ah-peh-ree-TEE-voh

a mixed drink
un combinado
oon kohm-bee-NAH-dhoh

some wine
un vino
oon VEE-noh

a soup
una sopa
OO-nah SOH-pah

an appetizer
un primer plato
oon pree-MEHR PLAH-toh

a salad
una ensalada
OO-nah ehn-sah-LAH-dhah

some bread
un pedazo de pan
oon peh-DHAH-thoh dheh pahn

a [main course / entrée]
un segundo plato
oon seh-GOON-doh PLAH-toh

a side dish
una guarnición
OO-nah gwahr-nee-thee-OHN

dessert
un postre
oon POHSS-treh

some fruit
fruta
FROO-tah

some cheese
queso
KEH-soh

a coffee
un café
oon kah-FEH

[anything / something] else
algo más
AHL-goh mahss

I like this.
Me gusta esto.
meh GOOSS-tah EHSS-toh.

I don't like that.
No me gusta eso.
noh meh GOOSS-tah EH-soh.

Wining & Dining ♥ Screen & Stage

Cheers!
¡Salud!
sah-LOODH!

Bon appétit.
Buen provecho.
bwehn proh-VEH-choh.

Let's split the check.
Dividimos la cuenta.
dee-vee-DHEE-mohss lah KWEHN-tah.

It's my treat.
Te invito yo.
teh een-VEE-toh yoh.

CAFES, BARS & DISCOS

SEE *BARS & DARK PLACES* (P. 17) AND *COCKTAILS FOR TWO* (P. 19).

SCREEN & STAGE

What movie's playing?
¿Qué película ponen?
keh peh-LEE-koo-lah POH-nehn?

What time does it start?
¿A qué hora empieza?
ah keh OH-rah ehm-pee-EH-thah?

SEE APPENDIX A: *CLOCKWISE* (P. 108).

Have you seen this one?
¿Has visto ésta?
ahss VEESS-toh EHSS-tah?

I've heard it's ... .
He oído que ... .
eh oh-EE-dhoh keh ... .

very good está muy bien *ehss-TAH mwee bee-EHN*	**funny** es graciosa *ehss grah-thee-OH-sah*
very long es muy larga *ehss mwee LAHR-gah*	**awful** es horrible *ehss oh-RREE-bleh*
fun es divertida *ehss dee-vehr-TEE-dhah*	**boring** es aburrida *ehss ah-boo-RREE-dhah*

It's in [Spanish / English].
Está en [español / inglés].
ehss-TAH ehn [ehss-pah-NYOHL / een-GLEHSS].

It's dubbed in [Spanish / English].
Está doblada al [español / inglés].
ehss-TAH dhoh-BLAH-dhah ahl [ehss-pah-NYOHL / een-GLEHSS].

It's subtitled.
Tiene subtítulos.
tee-EH-neh soop-TEE-too-lohss.

Do you like the ... ?
¿Te gusta ... ?
teh GOOSS-tah ... ?

[film / show]
[la película / el espectáculo]
lah peh-LEE-koo-lah /
ehl ehss-pehk-TAH-koo-loh]

[actor / actress]
[el actor / la actriz]
[ehl ahk-TOHR / lah ahk-TREETH]

director
[el director / la directora]
[ehl dee-rehk-TOHR /
lah dhee-rehk-TOH-rah]

story
el argumento
ehl ahr-goo-MEHN-toh

Would you like ... ?
¿Quieres ... ?
kee-EH-rehss ... ?

---

a drink	popcorn	candy
beber algo	palomitas	caramelos
beh-BEHR	*pah-loh-*	*kah-rah-*
AHL-goh	*MEE-tahss*	*MEH-lohss*

MUSIC, PLEASE

What's on the program?
¿Qué hay en el programa?
keh AH-ee ehn ehl
proh-GRAH-mah?

Who's the conductor?
¿Quién es [el director / la
directora]?
kee-EHN ehss [ehl dee-rehk-
TOHR / lah dhee-rehk-TOH-rah]?

Who's singing?
¿Quién canta?
kee-EHN KAHN-tah?

Do you know this ... ?
¿Conoces esta ... ?
koh-NOH-thehss EHSS-tah ... ?

---

work	piece	song
obra	pieza	canción
OH-brah	*pee-EH-*	*kahn-thee-*
	thah	*OHN*

It's beautiful.
Es muy bonita.
ehss mwee boh-NEE-tah.

It's (not) so great.
(No) es muy buena.
(noh) ehss mwee BWEH-nah.

Do you like the ... ?
¿Te gusta ... ?
teh GOOSS-tah ... ?

composer	conductor
[el compositor / la compositora] *[ehl kohm-poh-see-TOHR / lah kohm-poh-see-TOH-rah]*	[el director / la directora] *[ehl dee-rehk-TOHR / lah dhee-rehk-TOH-rah]*
band la banda *lah BAHN-dah*	**singer** [el / la] cantante *[ehl / lah] kahn-TAHN-teh*

[He / She] sings very well.
[Él / Ella] canta muy bien.
[ehl I EH-yah] KAHN-tah mwee bee-EHN.

[He / She / The band] plays very well.
[Él / Ella / La banda] toca muy bien.
[ehl / EH-yah / lah BAHN-dah] TOH-kah mwee bee-EHN.

THE PARTY LINE

Who's giving this party?
¿Quién da la fiesta?
kee-EHN dah lah fee-EHSS-tah?

The [guy / girl] over there.
[Aquel chico / Aquella chica].
[ah-KEHL CHEE-koh / ah-KEH-yah CHEE-kah].

I'll introduce you [to him / to her].
Te [lo / la] presento.
teh [loh / lah] preh-SEHN-toh.

SEE *INTRODUCTIONS* (P. 21).

Want [a drink / something to eat]?
¿Quieres [beber / comer] algo?
kee-EH-rehss [beh-BEHR / koh-MEHR] AHL-goh?

SEE *COCKTAILS FOR TWO* (P. 19).

Are you enjoying yourself?
¿Te diviertes?
teh dhee-vee-EHR-tehss?

I'm having a great time.
Me lo estoy pasando muy bien.
meh loh ehss-TOH-ee pah-SAHN-doh mwee bee-EHN.

I'd like to go home.
Quisiera ir a casa.
kee-see-EH-rah eer ah KAH-sah.

Let's say goodbye.
Vamos a despedirnos.
VAH-mohss ah dhehss-peh-DHEER-nohss.

ENDGAME

Did you enjoy the ... ?
¿Te gustó ... ?
teh gooss-TOH ... ?

dinner	concert
la cena	el concierto
lah THEH-nah	*ehl kohn-thee-EHR-toh*
[ride / drive]	
el paseo	**museum**
ehl pah-SEH-oh	el museo
	ehl moo-SEH-oh
disco	
la discoteca	**party**
lah dheess-koh-TEH-kah	la fiesta
	lah fee-EHSS-tah
movie	
la película	**picnic**
lah peh-LEE-koo-lah	el picnic
	ehl PEEK-neek
show	
el espectáculo	**beach**
ehl ehss-pehk-TAH-koo-loh	la playa
	lah PLAH-yah

It was [good / excellent].
Estuvo [bien / muy bien].
ehss-TOO-voh [bee-EHN / mwee bee-EHN].

It was [not so great / terrible].
[No fue gran cosa / Fue horrible].
[noh fweh grahn KOH-sah / fweh oh-RREE-bleh].

Want to go somewhere else?
¿Quieres ir a otro sitio?
kee-EH-rehss eer ah OH-troh SEE-tee-oh?

Let's go somewhere else.
Vamos a otro sitio.
VAH-mohss ah OH-troh SEE-tee-oh.

Where do you want to go?
¿Adónde quieres ir?
ah-DHON-deh kee-EH-rehss eer?

Let's go dancing.
Vamos a bailar.
VAH-mohss ah bah-ee-LAHR.

Let's go for a walk.
Vamos a dar un paseo.
VAH-mohss ah dhahr oon pah-SEH-oh.

Want to come over for a drink?
¿Quieres venir a casa a tomar algo?
kee-EH-rehss veh-NEER ah KAH-sah ah toh-MAHR AHL-goh?

SEE ALSO *MY PLACE OR YOURS* (P. 32).

Sure.
Con gusto.
kohn GOOSS-toh.

I should go home.
Tengo que volver a casa.
*TEHN-goh keh vohl-VEHR ah
KAH-sah.*

I'll take you home.
Te llevo a casa.
*teh YEH-voh ah
KAH-sah.*

SEE *SURE THING!* (P. 33),
SEE *YOU LATER* (P. 34),
OR *NO, THANKS* (P. 35).

May I come in?
¿Puedo entrar?
*PWEH-dhoh
ehn-TRAHR?*

**Want to come in
(for a while)?**
¿Quieres entrar
(un rato)?
*kee-EH-rehss
ehn-TRAHR (oon
RRAH-toh)?*

(I'm sorry,) I'm tired.
(Lo siento,) estoy [cansado /
cansada].
*(loh see-EHN-toh,) ehss-TOH-ee
[kahn-SAH-dhoh / kahn-SAH-dhah].*

**I'd like to see
you again.**
Quisiera
volverte a ver.
*kee-see-EH-rah
vohl-VEHR-teh
ah vehr.*

I have to get up early tomorrow.
Tengo que levantarme temprano
mañana.
*TEHN-goh keh leh-vahn-TAHR-
meh tehm-PRAH-noh mah-
NYAH-nah.*

(Thanks,) I've had a great time.
(Gracias,) me lo pasé muy bien.
*(GRAH-thee-ahss,) meh loh
pah-SEH mwee
bee-EHN.*

**I'll call you
[tomorrow / this
weekend].**
Te llamo [mañana /
este fin de semana].
*teh YAH-moh
[mah-NYAH-nah /
EHSS-teh feen
deh seh-MAH-
nah].*

SEE ALSO APPENDIX A:
WHEN? (P. 105).

How about a good-night kiss?
¿Me das un beso?
meh dhahss oon BEH-soh?

Next time.
La próxima vez.
lah PROHK-see-mah vehth.

Sex, Etc.

DIFFERENT STROKES

Only safe sex.
Sólo sexo seguro.
*SOH-loh SEHK-soh
seh-GOO-roh.*

What are you into?
¿Que te gusta hacer?
keh teh GOOSS-tah ah-THEHR?

I (don't) like ... .
(No) me gusta ... .
(noh) meh GOOSS-tah... .

to kiss besar *beh-SAHR*	**to suck cock** mamar *mah-MAHR*	**to be fucked** que me follen *keh meh FOH-yehn*
gentle sex la ternura *lah tehr-NOO-rah*	**to get sucked** que me la mamen *keh meh lah MAH-mehn*	**S & M** el sadomasoquismo *ehl sah-dhoh-mah-soh-KEESS-moh*
rough sex el sexo a lo duro *ehl SEHK-soh ah loh DHOO-roh*	**to get eaten out** que me lo coman *keh meh loh KOH-mahn*	**leather** el cuero *ehl KWEH-roh*
to masturbate [myself / you] [masturbarme / masturbarte] *[mahss-toor-BAHR-meh / mahss-toor-BAHR-teh]*	**to eat ass** lamer el culo *lah-MEHR ehl KOO-loh* **to get my ass eaten out** que me laman el culo *keh meh LAH-mahn ehl KOO-loh*	**to [tie my lover up / get tied up]** [atar / que me aten] *[ah-TAHR / keh meh AH-tehn]*
to eat pussy comer chocho *koh-MEHR CHOH-choh*	**to fuck** follar *foh-YAHR*	**bondage & discipline** la esclavitud y la disciplina *lah ehss-klah-vee-TOODH ee lah dheess-thee-PLEE-nah*

Different Strokes ♥ Let's Do It

I (don't) like [threeways / group sex].
(No) me gustan [los tríos / las orgías].
(noh) meh GOOSS-tahn [lohss TREE-ohss / lahss ohr-HEE-ahss].

That turns me on.
Eso me excita.
EH-soh meh ehks-THEE-tah.

I don't like that.
Eso no me gusta.
EH-soh noh meh GOOSS-tah.

That's unsafe.
Eso es peligroso.
EH-soh ehss peh-lee-GROH-soh.

I don't do that.
Yo no hago eso.
yoh noh AH-goh EH-soh.

I'd rather not.
Mejor que no.
meh-HOHR keh noh.

I've never done that.
Nunca he hecho eso.
NOON-kah eh EH-choh EH-soh.

But I'll try it.
Pero lo probaré.
PEH-roh loh proh-bah-REH.

Not without a condom.
No sin condón.
noh seen kohn-DOHN.

LET'S DO IT

I want to ... .
Quiero ... .
kee-EH-roh ... .

kiss you besarte *beh-SAHR-teh*	**make love to you** hacer el amor contigo *ah-THEHR ehl ah-MOHR kohn-TEE-goh*
touch you tocarte *toh-KAHR-teh*	
caress you acariciarte *ah-kah-ree-thee-AHR-teh*	**go to bed with you** acostarme contigo *ah-kohss-TAHR-meh kohn-TEE-goh*
put my arms around you abrazarte *ah-brah-THAHR-teh*	**fuck you** follarte *foh-YAHR-teh*
take your clothes off quitarte la ropa *kee-TAHR-te lah RROH-pah*	**have you inside me** tenerte dentro *teh-NEHR-teh DHEHN-troh*

NOT SO FAST

Wait.
Espera.
ehss-PEH-rah

Not so fast.
No tan de prisa.
noh tahn deh PREE-sah.

(Please) stop.
(Por favor,) para.
(pohr fah-VOHR,) PAH-rah.

Don't.
No hagas eso.
noh AH-gahss EH-soh.

What's wrong?
¿Qué pasa?
keh PAH-sah?

I'm nervous.
Estoy [nervioso / nerviosa].
ehss-TOH-ee [nehr-vee-OH-soh / nehr-vee-OH-sah].

It's too soon.
Me parece muy pronto.
meh pah-REH-theh mwee PROHN-toh.

This is my first time.
Es mi primera vez.
ehss mee pree-MEH-rah vehth.

I'm not very experienced.
No tengo mucha experiencia.
noh TEHN-goh MOO-chah ehks-peh-ree-EHN-thee-ah.

I'm a virgin.
Soy virgen.
SOH-ee VEER-hehn.

We'll go slow.
Iremos despacito.
ee-REH-mohss dehss-pah-THEE-toh.

Relax. It'll be all right.
Calma. No va a pasar nada.
KAHL-mah. noh vah ah pah-SAHR NAH-dhah.

If it hurts, I'll take it out.
Si te duele, te la saco.
see teh DHWEH-leh, teh lah SAH-koh.

I'm sorry. I can't do this.
Lo siento. No puedo hacerlo.
loh see-EHN-toh. noh PWEH-dhoh ah-THEHR-loh.

Not So Fast ♥ Practical Love

Don't go inside me.
No me penetres.
noh meh peh-NEH-trehss.

It's the wrong time of month.
Tengo la regla.
TEHN-goh lah RREH-glah.

Not tonight. I have a headache.
Esta noche no. Me duele la
cabeza.
*EHSS-tah NOH-cheh noh. meh
DHWEH-leh lah kah-BEH-thah.*

PRACTICAL LOVE

Do you have condoms?
¿Tienes condones?
tee-EH-nehss kohn-DOH-nehss?

I (don't) have condoms.
(No) tengo condones.
*(noh) TEHN-goh kohn-DOH-
nehss.*

Are you protected? *(to a woman)*
¿Vas segura?
vahss seh-GOO-rah?

I'm on the pill.
Tomo la píldora.
TOH-moh lah PEEL-doh-rah.

I have an IUD.
Tengo un DIU.
TEHN-goh oon deh-ee-OO.

(But) you have to use a condom.
(Pero) tienes que usar condón.
*(PEH-roh) tee-EH-nehss keh
oo-SAHR kohn-DOHN.*

I insist.
Insisto.
een-SEESS-toh.

Do you have [cream / lubricant]?
¿Tienes [crema / lubricante]?
*tee-EH-nehss [KREH-mah /
loo-bree-KAHN-teh]?*

I have to go to the bathroom.
Tengo que ir al baño.
TEHN-goh keh eer ahl BAH-nyoh.

I want to wash up first.
Quiero lavarme primero.
*kee-EH-roh lah-VAHR-meh
pree-MEH-roh.*

**Want to take a [shower / bath]
(together)?**
¿Quieres que nos [duchemos /
bañemos] (juntos)?
*kee-EH-rehss keh nohss
[doo-CHEH-mohss / bah-NYEH-
mohss] (HOON-tohss)?*

The Right Position

THE RIGHT POSITION

Stand up.
Levántate.
leh-VAHN-tah-teh.

Let's go to the bed.
Vamos a la cama.
VAH-mohss ah lah KAH-mah.

Lie down.
Acuéstate.
ah-KWEHSS-tah-teh.

Turn over.
Date la vuelta.
DAH-teh lah VWEHL-tah.

Move (a little) that way.
Échate (un poco) para allá.
EH-chah-teh (oon POH-koh) PAH-rah ah-YAH.

Don't move.
No te muevas.
noh teh MWEH-vahss.

Go on top.
Ponte encima.
POHN-teh ehn-THEE-mah.

Go on your side.
Ponte de lado.
POHN-teh dheh LAH-dhoh.

Go on your knees.
Ponte de rodillas.
POHN-teh dheh rroh-DHEE-yahss.

Go on the floor.
Ponte en el suelo.
POHN-teh ehn ehl SWEH-loh.

Raise your legs.
Levanta las piernas.
leh-VAHN-tah lahss pee-EHR-nahss.

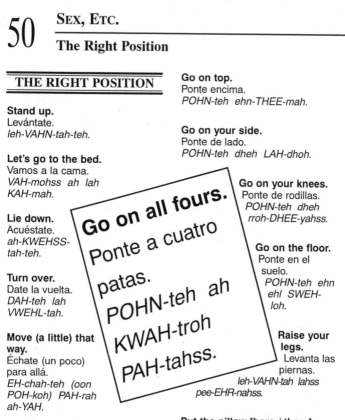

Go on all fours.
Ponte a cuatro patas.
POHN-teh ah KWAH-troh PAH-tahss.

Put the pillow [here / there].
Pon la almohada [aquí / ahí].
pohn lah ahl-MWAH-dhah [ah-KEE / ah-EE].

TOUCH, SQUEEZE & NIBBLE

Want a massage?
¿Quieres que te dé un masaje?
kee-EHR-ehss keh teh dheh oon mah-SAH-heh?

Do my ... .
Dámelo en ... .
DAH-meh-loh ehn ... .

back	**rear**
la espalda	las nalgas
lah ehss-PAHL-dah	*lahss NAHL-gahss*
shoulders	**legs**
los hombros	las piernas
lohss OHM-brohss	*lahss pee-EHR-nahss*
neck	**feet**
el cuello	los pies
ehl KWEH-yoh	*lohss pee-EHSS*

(A little) [harder / softer].
(Un poco) [más fuerte / más suave].
(oon POH-koh) [mahss FWEHR-teh / mahss SWAH-veh].

Does that feel good?
¿Te gusta?
teh GOOSS-tah?

That feels great.
Está muy bien.
ehss-TAH mwee bee-EHN.

You do that so well.
Qué bien lo haces.
keh bee-EHN loh AH-thehss.

Put your arms around me.
Abrázame.
ah-BRAH-thah-meh.

Take [my / your] clothes off.
[Quítame / Quítate] la ropa.
[KEE-tah-meh / KEE-tah-teh] lah RROH-pah.

Don't take [my / your] clothes off (yet).
No [me / te] quites la ropa (todavía).
noh [meh / teh] KEE-tehss lah RROH-pah (toh-dhah-VEE-ah).

Don't give me a hickey.
No me des un chupetón.
noh meh dhehss oon choo-peh-TOHN.

Touch, Squeeze & Nibble

Kiss [me / my ...].
Bésame ... .
BEH-sah-me ... .

Touch [me / my ...].
Tócame ... .
TOH-kah-meh ... .

Caress [me / my ...].
Acaríciame ... .
ah-kah-REE-thee-ah-meh ... .

Rub [me / my ...].
Frótame ... .
FROH-tah-meh ... .

Play with [me / my ...].
[Juega conmigo /
Juguetéame con ...].
[HWEH-gah kohn-MEE-goh / hoo-geh-TEH-ah-meh kohn ...].

Lick [me / my ...].
Lámeme ... .
LAH-meh-meh ... .

**Bite [me / my ...]
[hard / gently].**
Muérdeme ...
[fuerte / suave].
*MWEHR-dheh-meh ...
[FWEHR-teh / SWAH-veh].*

Pinch [me / my ...].
Pellízcame ... .
peh-YEETH-kah-meh ... .

MIX & MATCH!
"LICK ME" IS LÁMEME,
AND "LICK MY EARS" IS
LÁMEME LAS OREJAS.

Squeeze [me / my ...].
Apriétame ... .
ah-pree-EH-tah-meh ... .

---

hair
el pelo
ehl PEH-loh

ears
las orejas
lahss oh-REH-hahss

lips
los labios
lohss LAH-bee-ohss

neck
el cuello
ehl KWEH-yoh

breasts
el pecho
ehl PEH-choh

tits
las tetas
lahss TEH-tahss

nipples
los pezones
lohss peh-THOH-nehss

armpits
los sobacos
lohss soh-BAH-kohss

hands
las manos
lahss MAH-nohss

fingers
los dedos
lohss DEH-dhohss

pussy
el chocho
ehl CHOH-choh

clit(oris)
el clítoris
ehl KLEE-toh-reess

cock
la polla
lah POH-yah

foreskin
el prepucio
ehl preh-POO-thee-oh

balls
los huevos
lohss WEH-vohss

ass (hole)
el (ojo del) culo
ehl (OH-hoh dhehl) KOO-loh

[legs / thighs]
[las piernas / los muslos]
[lahss pee-EHR-nahss / lohss MOOSS-lohss]

feet
los pies
lohss pee-EHSS

toes
los dedos de los pies
lohss DEH-dhohss deh lohss pee-EHSS

Touch, Squeeze & Nibble ♥ Fun With Fingers

Kiss me (down there).
Bésame (por ahí).
BEH-sah-meh (pohr ah-EE).

Touch me (here).
Tócame (aquí).
TOH-kah-meh (ah-KEE).

Don't touch me (there).
No me toques (ahí).
noh meh TOH-kehss (ah-EE).

You're tickling me!
¡Me haces cosquillas!
meh AH-thehss kohss-KEE-yahss!

Don't tickle me.
No me hagas cosquillas.
noh meh AH-gahss kohss-KEE-yahss.

Don't do that!
¡No hagas eso!
noh AH-gahss EH-soh!

Make me come.
Haz que me corra.
AHTH keh meh KOH-rrah.

Don't make me come (yet).
No hagas que me corra (todavía).
noh AH-gahss keh meh KOH-rrah (toh-dhah-VEE-ah).

FUN WITH FINGERS

Put your finger inside [me / my pussy / my ass].
Méteme un dedo [... / en el chocho / en el culo].
MEH-teh-meh oon DEH-dhoh [... / ehn ehl CHOH-choh / ehn ehl KOO-loh].

Deeper.
Más dentro.
mahss DEHN-troh.

More (fingers).
Más (dedos).
mahss (DEH-dhohss).

(Hey,) not so many.
(Oye,) no tantos.
(OH-yeh,) noh TAHN-tohss.

Take them out.
Sácalos.
SAH-kah-lohss.

SEE ALSO *OUCH!* (P. 67).

ORAL EXERCISES

Put it in my mouth.
Pónmela en la boca.
POHN-meh-lah ehn lah BOH-kah.

Take it in your mouth.
Métetela en la boca.
MEH-teh-teh-lah ehn lah BOH-kah.

Suck [me / my tits / my cock].
Chúpame [... / las tetas / la polla].
CHOO-pah-me [... / lahss TEH-tahss / lah POH-yah].

Eat [it *(cunt or cock)* / me].
[Cómemelo / Cómeme].
[KOH-meh-meh-loh / KOH-meh-meh].

Eat my cock.
Cómeme la polla.
KOH-meh-meh lah POH-yah.

[Blow me / Give me head].
Mámamela.
MAH-mah-meh-lah.

Lick it.
Lámela.
LAH-meh-lah.

Take my balls in your mouth.
Chúpame los huevos.
CHOO-pah-meh lohss WEH-vohss.

I want ... .
Quiero ... .
kee-EH-roh ... .

to take it in my mouth	you to eat me out
metérmela en la boca	que me lo comas
meh-TEHR-meh-lah ehn lah BOH-kah	*keh meh loh KOH-mahss*
to put it in your mouth	**you to suck me**
metértela en la boca	que me la chupes
meh-TEHR-teh-lah ehn lah BOH-kah	*keh meh lah CHOO-pehss*
to eat you out	**to suck you**
comértelo	chupártela
koh-MEHR-teh-loh	*choo-PAHR-teh-lah*
	to fuck your face
	follarte por la boca
	foh-YAHR-teh pohr lah BOH-kah

Fuck my face.
Fóllame por la boca.
FOH-yah-meh pohr lah BOH-kah.

Sit on my face.
Ponme el culo en la cara.
POHN-meh ehl KOO-loh ehn lah KAH-rah.

Eat my ass.
Cómeme el culo.
KOH-meh-meh ehl KOO-loh.

Turn around.
Date la vuelta.
DAH-teh lah VWEHL-tah.

Let's sixty-nine.
Vamos a hacer un sesenta y nueve.
VAH-mohss ah ah-THEHR oon seh-SEHN-tah ee NWEH-veh.

[Faster / Slower].
Más [rápido / lento].
mahss [RRAH-pee-dhoh / LEHN-toh].

Take it all the way.
Trágatela.
TRAH-gah-teh-lah.

I can't. It's too big.
No puedo. Es demasiado grande.
noh PWEH-dhoh. ehss deh-mah-see-AH-dhoh GRAHN-deh.

I'm gagging.
Me ahogo.
meh ah-OH-goh.

Watch your teeth.
Cuidado con los dientes.
kwee-DHAH-dhoh kohn lohss dee-EHN-tehss.

Don't come in my mouth.
Córrete fuera.
KOH-rreh-teh FWEH-rah.

I won't come in your mouth.
Me correré fuera.
meh koh-rreh-REH FWEH-rah.

Tell me when you're going to come.
Dime cuando te vayas a correr.
DEE-meh KWAHN-doh teh VAH-yahss ah koh-RREHR.

Stop. I want you inside.
Para. Te quiero adentro.
PAH-rah. teh kee-EH-roh ah-DHEHN-troh.

I want you to [take / fuck] me.
Quiero que me [tomes / folles].
kee-EH-roh keh meh [TOH-mehss / FOH-yehss].

THE MAIN EVENT

HE

I want to take you.
Quiero tomarte.
kee-EH-roh toh-MAHR-teh.

Let me do it to you.
Déjame hacértelo.
DEH-hah-meh ah-THEHR-teh-loh.

I want to put it inside you.
Quiero penetrarte.
kee-EH-roh peh-neh-TRAHR-teh.

I want to fuck you.
Quiero follarte.
kee-EH-roh foh-YAHR-teh.

Can I?
¿Puedo?
PWEH-dhoh?

I'll be gentle.
Voy a ser suave.
VOH-ee ah sehr SWAH-veh.

Are you ready?
¿Estás lista?
ehss-TAHSS LEESS-tah?

SHE

Take me.
Tómame.
TOH-mah-meh.

Do it to me.
Házmelo.
AHTH-meh-loh.

Put it inside me.
Penétrame.
peh-NEH-trah-meh.

Fuck me.
Fóllame.
FOH-yah-meh.

[You can / Don't].
[Puedes / No].
[PWEH-dhehss / noh].

Please be gentle.
Sé suave.
seh SWAH-veh.

I'm (not) ready.
(No) estoy lista.
(noh) ehss-TOH-ee LEESS-tah.

HE

SHE

You need more [cream / lubricant].
Hace falta más [crema / lubricante].
AH-theh FAHL-tah mahss
[KREH-mah / loo-bree-KAHN-teh].

Put (more) cream on [me / yourself].
[Ponme / Ponte] (más) crema.
[POHN-meh / POHN-teh]
(mahss) KREH-mah.

Put a condom on me.
Ponme un condón.
POHN-meh oon kohn-DOHN.

Put on a condom.
Ponte un condón.
POHN-teh oon kohn-DOHN.

Spread your legs.
Ábrete de piernas.
AH-breh-teh dheh pee-EHR-nahss.

Put your legs around my waist.
Abrázame con las piernas.
ah-BRAH-thah-meh kohn lahss pee-EHR-nahss.

Spread my legs.
Ábreme las piernas.
AH-breh-meh lahss pee-EHR-nahss.

How do you want it?
¿Cómo lo hacemos?
KOH-moh loh ah-THEH-mohss?

Any way you want.
Como quieras.
KOH-moh kee-EH-rahss.

OR... SEE NEXT PAGE!

STOP IT RIGHT NOW.
(and read *AIDS Update* on page 10!)

The Main Event

HE

SHE

I want to do it ... .
Quiero hacerlo ... .
kee-EH-roh ah-THEHR-loh ... .

I want you to do it ... .
Quiero que lo hagas ... .
kee-EH-roh keh loh AH-gahss ... .

on [your / my] back [contigo / conmigo] boca arriba *[kohn-TEE-goh / kohn-MEE-goh] BOH-kah ah-RREE-bah*	**[doggy style / on all fours]** a cuatro patas *ah KWAH-troh PAH-tahss*	**in the [shower / bath / water]** en [la ducha / la bañera / el agua] *ehn [lah DOO-chah / lah bah-NYEH-rah / ehl AH-gwah]*
	standing up de pie *dheh pee-EH*	
on [your / my] stomach [contigo / conmigo] boca abajo *[kohn-TEE-goh / kohn-MEE-goh] BOH-kah ah-BAH-hoh*	**on the bed** en la cama *ehn lah KAH-mah*	**outside** afuera *ah-FWEH-rah*
on [your / my] side de lado *dheh LAH-dhoh*	**on the [floor / ground]** en el suelo *ehn ehl SWEH-loh*	**on the [grass / sand]** en [el cesped / la arena] *ehn [ehl THEHSS-pehdh / lah ah-REH-nah]*
on [your/ my] knees de rodillas *dheh rroh-DHEE-yahss*	**on the table** en la mesa *ehn lah MEH-sah*	**in the car** en el coche *ehn ehl KOH-cheh*

Let's try another way.
Vamos a probar de otra manera.
VAH-mohss ah proh-BAHR dheh OH-trah mah-NEH-rah.

Can we try another way?
¿Probamos de otra manera?
proh-BAH-mohss deh OH-trah mah-NEH-rah?

Get on top.
Ponte encima.
POHN-teh ehn-THEE-mah.

I'll get on top.
Me pongo encima.
meh POHN-goh ehn-THEE-mah.

HE	**SHE**
Sit on my cock. Siéntateme en la polla. *see-EHN-tah-teh-meh ehn lah POH-yah.*	**I want to sit on your cock.** Quiero sentarme en tu polla. *kee-EH-roh sehn-TAHR-meh ehn too POH-yah.*
I'm going in. Voy a entrar. *VOH-ee ah ehn-TRAHR.*	**Go in [slow / fast].** Penétrame [suave / fuerte]. *peh-NEH-trah-meh [SWAH-veh / FWEHR-teh].*
I'm going in deep. Voy hasta el fondo. *VOH-ee AHSS-tah ehl FOHN-doh.*	**Go in deep.** Ve hasta el fondo. *VEH AHSS-tah ehl FOHN-doh.*
I'm going to fuck you hard. Te voy a follar a lo duro. *teh VOH-ee ah foh-YAHR ah loh DHOO-roh.*	**[Fuck me / Don't fuck me] hard.** [Fóllame / No me folles] a lo duro. *[FOH-yah-meh / noh meh FOH-yehss] ah loh DHOO-roh.*
You want more? ¿Quieres más? *kee-EH-rehss mahss?*	**[I want more / Stop].** [Sigue / Para]. *[SEE-gheh / PAH-rah].*
I want to take you "back there." *(anal intercourse)* Te quiero follar por detrás. *teh kee-EH-roh foh-YAHR pohr dheh-TRAHSS.*	**Fuck me "back there."** Fóllame por detrás. *FOH-yah-meh pohr dheh-TRAHSS.* SEE ALSO *NOT SO FAST* (P. 48).

SEE ALSO *NOT SO FAST* (P. 48).

CRIES OF PASSION

Yes!
¡Sí!
see!

More!
¡Más!
mahss!

Do it.
Hazlo.
AHTH-loh.

Deeper!
¡Más dentro!
mahss DEHN-troh!

Harder!
¡Más fuerte!
mahss FWEHR-teh!

Don't (ever) stop.
No pares (nunca).
noh PAH-rehss (NOON-kah).

Is that good?
¿Te gusta?
teh GOOSS-tah?

(Yeah,) that's good.
(Sí,) me gusta.
(see,) meh GOOSS-tah.

You like that?
¿Te va eso?
teh vah EH-soh?

(Yes,) I like that (a lot).
(Sí,) me va (cantidad).
(see,) meh vah (kahn-tee-DHADH).

You like it, don't you?
¿A que te gusta?
ah keh teh GOOSS-tah?

That feels great.
Me encanta.
meh ehn-KAHN-tah.

I'm so hot.
Estoy muy caliente.
ehss-TOH-ee mwee kah-lee-EHN-teh.

You get me so hot.
Me estás poniendo caliente.
meh ehss-TAHSS poh-nee-EHN-doh kah-lee-EHN-teh.

You're driving me wild.
Me estás volviendo [loco / loca].
meh ehss-TAHSS vohl-vee-EHN-doh [LOH-koh / LOH-kah].

Talk dirty to me.
Dime porquerías.
DEE-meh pohr-keh-REE-ahss.

Don't be gross.
No seas [grosero / grosera].
noh SEH-ahss [groh-SEH-roh / groh-SEH-rah].

You're a great cocksucker.
¡Qué bien la chupas!
keh bee-EHN lah CHOO-pahss!

You're a great fucker.
Jodes de fábula.
HOH-dhehss dheh FAH-boo-lah.

You're so ... .
¡Qué ... tienes!
keh ... tee-EH-nehss!

tight	wet
estrecho lo	mojado lo
ehss-TREH-choh loh	*moh-HAH-dhoh loh*
hard	thick
tiesa la	gorda la
tee-EH-sah lah	*GOHR-dhah lah*

I'm so wet.
Lo tengo empapado.
loh TEHN-goh ehm-pah-PAH-dhoh.

I'm so hard.
La tengo muy tiesa.
lah TEHN-goh mwee tee-EH-sah.

It feels so good in there.
Qué bien encajamos.
keh bee-EHN ehn-kah-HAH-mohss.

You animal!
¡Eres un animal!
EH-rehss oon ah-nee-MAHL!

You savage!
¡Salvaje!
sahl-VAH-heh!

You beast!
¡Bestia!
BEHSS-tee-ah!

What a hot stud!
¡Qué calentón!
keh kah-lehn-TOHN!

You horny bastard!
¡Cachondo!
kah-CHOHN-doh!

(Shit,) you're a sex machine!
¡(Coño,) eres una máquina de joder!
(KOH-nyoh,) EH-rehss OO-nah MAH-kee-nah dheh hoh-DHEHR!

You hot lady!
¡Calentorra!
kah-lehn-TOH-rrah!

You nympho!
¡Ninfómana!
neen-FOH-mah-nah!

You slut!
¡Guarra!
GWAH-rrah!

You hot bitch!
¡Cachonda!
kah-CHOHN-dah!

You whore!
¡Puta!
POO-tah!

SEE ALSO *TERMS OF ENDEARMENT* (P. 80).

COMING

Slow down.
Más lento.
mahss LEHN-toh.

Stop!
¡Para!
PAH-rah!

Wait!
¡Espera!
ehss-PEH-rah!

I'm getting close.
Estoy llegando.
ehss-TOH-ee yeh-GAHN-doh.

I'm going to come!
¡Me voy a correr!
meh VOH-ee ah koh-RREHR!

I want to come inside you.
Quiero correrme dentro de ti.
kee-EH-roh koh-RREHR-meh
DHEHN-troh dheh tee.

[Come / Don't come] inside me.
[Córreteme / No te me corras]
dentro.
[KOH-rreh-teh-me / noh teh meh
KOH-rrahss] DHEHN-troh.

CONDOMS HAVE BEEN KNOWN TO BREAK.
TELL HIM TO PULL OUT BEFORE HE COMES!

Pull out [now / before you come].
Sácala [ahora / antes de correrte].
SAH-kah-lah [ah-OH-rah / AHN-
tehss deh koh-RREHR-teh].

Coming ♥ Getting Kinky: Tying Things Up

I'm coming!
¡Me estoy corriendo!
*meh ehss-TOH-ee
koh-rree-EHN-doh!*

Come on ... .
Córreteme en ... .
KOH-rreh-teh-meh ehn ... .

I want to come on ... .
Quiero correrme en ... .
*kee-EH-roh koh-RREHR-meh
ehn ... .*

[my / your] chest	[my / your] back
[el / tu] pecho	[la / tu] espalda
[ehl / too] PEH-choh	*[lah / too] ehss-PAHL-dah*

[my / your] tits	[my / your] face
[las / tus] tetas	[la / tu] cara
[lahss / tooss] TEH-tahss	*[lah / too] KAH-rah*

Did you come?
¿Te has corrido?
teh ahss koh-RREE-dhoh?

Want to clean up?
¿Quieres lavarte?
kee-EH-rehss lah-VAHR-teh?

I need to clean up.
Necesito lavarme.
neh-theh-SEE-toh lah-VAHR-meh.

GETTING KINKY

TYING THINGS UP

Get [some rope / some stockings / a scarf].
Trae [una cuerda / unas medias / una bufanda].
TRAH-eh [OO-nah KWEHR-dhah / OO-nahss MEH-dhee-ahss / OO-nah boo-FAHN-dah].

I'm going to tie you up.
Te voy a atar.
teh VOH-ee ah ah-TAHR.

Tie me up.
Átame.
AH-tah-meh.

Don't tie me up.
No me ates.
noh meh AH-tehss.

Untie me.
Desátame.
dehss-AH-tah-meh.

I'm going to handcuff you.
Te voy a poner las esposas.
teh VOH-ee ah poh-NEHR lahss ehss-POH-sahss.

Getting Kinky: Tying Things Up

Handcuff me.
Ponme las esposas.
POHN-meh lahss ehss-POH-sahss.

(Please) no handcuffs.
(Por favor) las esposas no.
(pohr fah-VOHR,) lahss ehss-POH-sahss noh.

Take the handcuffs off.
Quítame las esposas.
KEE-tah-meh lahss ehss-POH-sahss.

I'm going to gag you.
Te voy a amordazar.
teh VOH-ee ah ah-mohr-dah-THAHR.

(Please) don't gag me.
(Por favor,) amordazarme no.
(pohr fah-VOHR) ah-mohr-dah-THAHR-meh noh.

I'm going to blindfold you.
Te voy a vendar los ojos.
teh VOH-ee ah vehn-DAHR lohss OH-hohss.

Don't blindfold me.
No me vendes los ojos.
noh meh VEHN-dehss lohss OH-hohss.

Take the blindfold off (now).
Quítame las vendas (ahora).
KEE-tah-meh lahss VEHN-dahss (ah-OH-rah).

That's enough.
Basta ya.
BAHSS-tah yah.

Trust me.
Fíate de mí.
FEE-ah-teh dheh mee.

INTO HEAVIER SCENES? USE A **CODE WORD** TO STOP THE GAMES!

Stop if I say _____ , (okay?)
Para si digo _____ , (¿vale?)
PAH-rah see DEE-goh _____ , (VAH-leh?)

THE MORE THE MERRIER

Kiss [him / her / us].
[Bésalo / Bésala / Bésanos].
[BEH-sah-loh / BEH-sah-lah / BEH-sah-nohss].

Take [his / her] clothes off.
Quítale la ropa.
KEE-tah-leh lah RROH-pah.

Play with his cock.
Juega con su polla.
HWEH-gah kohn soo POH-yah.

Getting Kinky: The More The Merrier

Stroke his balls.
Acaríciale los huevos.
ah-kah-REE-thee-ah-leh lohss WEH-vohss.

Play with her tits.
Juega con sus tetas.
HWEH-gah kohn sooss TEH-tahss

Play with her nipples.
Juega con sus pezones.
HWEH-gah kohn sooss peh-THOH-nehss.

Finger her (pussy).
Métele un dedo (en el chocho).
MEH-teh-leh oon deh-dhoh (ehn ehl CHOH-choh).

Fuck her with the dildo.
Métele el consolador.
MEH-teh-leh ehl kohn-soh-lah-DHOHR.

Eat [her pussy / his cock].
Cómele [el chocho / la polla].
KOH-meh-leh [ehl CHOH-choh / lah POH-yah].

Suck [her tits / his cock].
Mámale [las tetas / la polla].
MAH-mah-leh [lahss TEH-tahss / lah POH-yah].

Lick [her slit / her cunt / his balls].
Lámele [la raja / el chocho / los huevos].
LAH-meh-leh [lah RRAH-hah / ehl CHOH-choh / lohss WEH-vohss].

Put a condom on his cock.
Ponle un condón en la polla.
POHN-leh oon kohn-DOHN ehn lah POH-yah.

Who wants it first?
¿Quién va primero?
kee-EHN vah pree-MEH-roh?

Take me first.
Fóllame primero a mí.
FOH-yah-meh pree-MEH-roh ah mee.

Take her first.
Fóllala primero a ella.
FOH-yah-lah pree-MEH-roh ah EH-yah.

Getting Kinky: The More the Merrier

Let's play "harem."
Vamos a jugar al "harén."
VAH-mohss ah hoo-GAHR ahl
"ah-REHN."

Sit on his cock.
Siéntatele en la polla.
see-EHN-tah-teh-leh ehn
lah POH-yah.

Fuck her.
Fóllala.
FOH-yah-lah.

Watch	Play with her tits
Mira	Acaríciale las tetas
MEE-rah	*ah-kah-REE-thee-ah-leh lahss TEH-tahss*
Kiss her	
Bésala	
BEH-sah-lah	

... while I fuck her.
... mientras la follo.
... mee-EHN-trahss lah FOH-yoh.

Take her while I watch.
Fóllala, que yo miro.
FOH-yah-lah, keh yoh MEE-roh.

Let's see you sixty-nine.
Haced un sesenta y nueve.
ah-THEHDH oon seh-SEHN-tah
ee NWEH-veh.

Let's take her together.
Vamos a follarla juntos.
VAH-mohss ah foh-YAHR-lah
HOON-tohss.

Let's make a "sandwich."
Vamos a hacer un "sandwich."
VAH-mohss ah ah-THEHR oon
"SAHND-weech."

Kiss [her / him] while I fuck you.
[Bésala / Bésalo] mientras te follo.
[BEH-sah-lah / BEH-sah-loh]
mee-EHN-trahss teh FOH-yoh.

Let's all kiss.
¡A besarse todos!
ah beh-SAHR-seh TOH-dhohss!

Getting Kinky: A Firm Hand ♥ Ouch!

A FIRM HAND

You need ... .
Te hace falta ... .
teh AH-theh FAHL-tah ... .

I need ... .
Me hace falta ... .
meh AH-theh FAHL-tah ... .

discipline
disciplina
dheess-thee-PLEE-nah

to be punished
ser [castigado / castigada]
sehr [kahss-tee-GAH-dhoh / kahss-tee-GAH-dhah]

a good beating
una buena paliza
OO-nah BWEH-nah pah-LEE-thah

I'm going to whip [you / your ass].
Te voy a azotar [... / en el culo].
teh VOH-ee ah ah-thoh-TAHR [... / ehn ehl KOO-loh].

[Hit me / Don't hit me].
[Pégame / No me pegues].
[PEH-gah-meh / noh meh PEH-ghehss].

[Whip me / Don't whip me].
[Azótame / No me azotes].
[ah-THOH-tah-meh / noh meh ah-THOH-tehss].

[Spank me / Don't spank me].
[Pégame / No me pegues] en el culo.
[PEH-gah-me / noh meh PEH-ghehss] ehn ehl KOO-loh.

[Slap me / Don't slap me].
[Dame / No me des] bofetadas.
[DAH-meh / noh meh dhehss] boh-feh-TAH-dhahss.

[Hurt me / Don't hurt me].
[Hazme / No me hagas] daño].
[AHTH-meh / noh meh AH-gahss] DAH-nyoh.

OUCH!

Are you all right?
¿Te encuentras bien?
teh ehn-KWEHN-trahss bee-EHN?

I'm (not) all right.
(No) me encuentro bien.
(noh) meh ehn-KWEHN-troh bee-EHN.

Is that too much?
¿Me estoy pasando?
meh ehss-TOH-ee pah-SAHN-doh?

It's too much.
Te has pasado.
teh ahss pah-SAH-dhoh.

You're going too far.
Te estás pasando.
teh ehss-TAHSS pah-SAHN-doh.

Not so hard!
¡No tan fuerte!
noh tahn FWEHR-teh!

Take it out.
Sácala.
SAH-kah-lah.

Don't do that.
No hagas eso.
noh AH-gahss EH-soh.

Am I hurting you?
¿Te estoy haciendo daño?
teh ehss-TOH-ee ah-thee-EHN-doh DHAH-nyoh?

You're (not) hurting me.
(No) me estás haciendo daño.
(noh) meh ehss-TAHSS ah-thee-EHN-doh DHAH-nyoh.

That hurts.
Me duele.
meh DHWEH-leh.

It's too big.
Es demasiado grande.
ehss deh-mah-see-AH-dhoh GRAHN-deh.

(But) don't stop.
(Pero) sigue.
(PEH-roh) SEE-gheh.

I'm (not) comfortable.
(No) estoy [cómodo / cómoda].
(noh) ehss-TOH-ee [KOH-moh-dhoh / KOH-moh-dhah].

I can take it.
Puedo seguir.
PWEH-dhoh seh-GHEER.

I can't take it.
No puedo más.
noh PWEH-dhoh mahss.

Ouch! ♥ Pecker Problems

Want to stop (for a while)?
¿Quieres parar (un rato)?
*kee-EH-rehss pah-RAHR
(oon RRAH-toh)?*

Let's stop (for a while).
Vamos a parar (un rato).
*VAH-mohss ah pah-RAHR
(oon RRAH-toh).*

Please stop!
¡Por favor, para!
pohr fah-VOHR, PAH-rah!

You're raping me!
¡Me estás violando!
*meh ehss-TAHSS
vee-oh-LAHN-doh!*

I mean it!
¡En serio!
ehn SEH-ree-oh!

I'll scream.
Voy a gritar.
VOH-ee ah gree-TAHR.

I'm going to call the police.
Voy a llamar a la policia.
*VOH-ee ah yah-MAHR ah lah
poh-lee-THEE-ah.*

I'll kick you in the balls!
¡Te voy a dar una patada en los
cojones!
*teh VOH-ee ah dhahr OO-nah
pah-TAH-dhah ehn lohss
koh-HOH-nehss!*

PECKER PROBLEMS

(I'm sorry,) I can't get it up.
(Lo siento,) no se me levanta.
*(loh see-EHN-toh,) noh seh
meh leh-VAHN-tah.*

**I don't know what's wrong
with me.**
No sé qué me pasa.
noh seh keh meh PAH-sah.

**I'm a little [nervous / tense /
tired].**
Estoy un poco [nervioso / tenso /
cansado].
*ehss-TOH-ee oon POH-koh
[nehr-vee-OH-soh / TEHN-soh /
kahn-SAH-dhoh].*

I drank too much.
Bebí demasiado.
beh-BEE dheh-mah-see-AH-dhoh.

Pecker Problems ♥ Stay or Go

I don't feel well.
No me siento bien.
noh meh see-EHN-toh bee-EHN.

It's not you.
No es culpa tuya.
noh ehss KOOL-pah TOO-yah.

No problem.
No importa.
noh eem-POHR-tah.

Don't worry.
No te preocupes.
noh teh preh-oh-KOO-pehss.

Let's just cuddle.
Vamos a acurrucarnos.
VAH-mohss ah ah-koo-rroo-KAHR-nohss.

Let's rest (a while).
Vamos a descansar (un rato).
VAH-mohss ah dhehss-kahn-SAHR (oon RRAH-toh).

We'll try again (later).
Lo intentaremos otra vez (luego).
loh een-tehn-tah-REH-mohss OH-trah vehth (LWEH-goh).

STAY OR GO

Would you like to stay over?
¿Te gustaría quedarte?
teh gooss-tah-REE-ah keh-DHAHR-teh?

May I stay over?
¿Puedo quedarme?
PWEH-dhoh keh-DHAHR-meh?

I'd love to.
Me encantaría.
meh ehn-kahn-tah-REE-ah.

I'd better go.
Mejor que me vaya.
meh-HOHR keh meh VAH-yah.

(I'm sorry, but) you'd better go.
(Lo siento, pero) mejor que te vayas.
(loh see-EHN-toh, PEH-roh) meh-HOHR keh teh VAH-yahss.

Don't be offended.
No te ofendas.
noh teh oh-FEHN-dahss.

I have things to do.
Tengo cosas que hacer.
TEHN-goh KOH-sahss keh ah-THEHR.

Stay or Go ♥ Zzzzz...

Someone is coming over soon.
Alguien va a llegar pronto.
AHL-ghee-ehn vah ah
yeh-GAHR PROHN-toh.

You have to leave ... .
Tienes que irte ... .
tee-EH-nehss keh EER-teh ... .

now	by 9:00 (in the morning)
ahora	antes de las
ah-OH-rah	nueve (de la
	mañana)
by midnight	*AHN-tehss deh*
antes de las doce	*lahss NWEH-veh*
AHN-tehss deh	*(dheh lah mah-*
lahss DOH-theh	*NYAH-nah)*

SEE ALSO APPENDIX A: *CLOCKWISE*
(P. 108).

Can you call me a taxi?
¿Me pides un taxi?
meh PEE-dhehss oon TAHK-see?

I'll drive you.
Te llevo yo.
teh YEH-voh yoh.

═══════════════════
ZZZZZ...
═══════════════════

Are you tired?
¿Estás [cansado / cansada]?
ehs-TAHSS [kahn-SAH-dhoh /
kahn-SAH-dhah]?

I'm tired.
Estoy [cansado / cansada].
ehs-TOH-ee [kahn-SAH-dhoh /
kahn-SAH-dhah].

I'm sleepy.
Tengo sueño.
TEHN-goh SWEH-nyoh.

Let's go to sleep.
Vamos a dormir.
VAH-mohss ah dhohr-MEER.

Good night.
Hasta mañana.
AHSS-tah mah-NYAH-nah.

A goodnight kiss.
Un beso.
oon BEH-soh.

Sleep well.
Que duermas bien.
keh DHWEHR-mahss bee-EHN.

Sweet dreams.
Que sueñes con los angelitos.
keh SWEH-nyehss kohn lohss
ahn-heh-LEE-tohss.

You, too.
Tú también.
too tahm-bee-EHN.

The Morning After

RISE & SHINE

Good morning.
Buenos días.
BWEH-nohss DEE-ahss.

Time to get up!
¡Es hora de
levantarse!
*ehss OH-rah
dheh leh-vahn-
TAHR-seh!*

What's your name, again?
¿Cómo te llamas?
*KOH-moh teh
YAH-mahss?*

Did you sleep well?
¿Dormiste bien?
dohr-MEESS-teh bee-EHN?

I feel great this morning.
Me siento muy bien esta mañana.
*meh see-EHN-toh mwee bee-
EHN EHSS-tah mah-NYAH-nah.*

I have a terrible hangover.
Qué resaca tengo.
keh rreh-SAH-kah TEHN-goh.

Who are you?
¿Quién eres?
kee-EHN EH-rehss?

What happened last night?
¿Qué pasó anoche?
keh pah-SOH ah-NOH-cheh?

We had a wonderful time.
Nos lo pasamos muy bien.
*nohss loh pah-SAH-mohss
mwee bee-EHN.*

Was it good for you?
¿Te lo pasaste bien?
*teh loh pah-SAHSS-teh
bee-EHN?*

It was great. And you?
Fue magnífico. ¿Y tú?
*fweh mahg-NEE-fee-
koh. ee too?*

I don't remember.
No me acuerdo.
noh meh ah-KWEHR-dhoh.

SOAP & WATER

Want to take a [shower / bath]?
¿Quieres [ducharte / bañarte]?
*kee-EH-rehss [doo-CHAHR-teh /
bah-NYAHR-teh]?*

Soap & Water ♥ Breaking the Fast ♥ And Now What?

Let's take a [shower / bath] (together).
Vamos a [ducharnos / bañarnos] (juntos).
VAH-mohss ah [dhoo-CHAHR-nohss / bah-NYAHR-nohss] (HOON-tohss).

Where's the bathroom?
¿Dónde está el baño?
DOHN-deh ehss-TAH ehl BAH-nyoh?

The bathroom is [here / there].
El baño está [aquí / allí].
ehl BAH-nyoh ehss-TAH [ah-KEE / ah-YEE].

SEE ALSO APPENDIX A: *WHERE?* (P. 106).

Do you have [a towel / soap]?
¿Tienes [una toalla / jabón]?
tee-EH-nehss [OO-nah toh-AH-yah / hah-BOHN]?

BREAKING THE FAST

Let's get breakfast (out).
Vamos a desayunar (fuera).
VAH-mohss ah dheh-sah-yoo-NAHR (FWEH-rah).

I'll make breakfast.
Yo preparo el desayuno.
yoh preh-PAH-roh ehl deh-sah-YOO-noh.

I'll serve you breakfast in bed.
Te sirvo el desayuno en la cama.
teh SEER-voh ehl deh-sah-YOO-noh ehn lah KAH-mah.

Let's get breakfast from room service.
Vamos a pedir el desayuno.
VAH-mohss ah peh-DHEER ehl deh-sah-YOO-noh.

AND NOW WHAT?

Would you like to spend the day together?
¿Te gustaría pasar el día juntos?
teh gooss-tah-REE-ah pah-SAHR ehl DEE-ah HOON-tohss?

I'd love to.
Me encantaría.
meh ehn-kahn-tah-REE-ah.

SEE ALSO *STAY OR GO* (P. 70) AND *SEE YOU LATER* (P. 34).

Sweet Talk

MUTUAL ADMIRATION SOCIETY

I like *you* a lot too.
Tú me gustas mucho también.
*too meh GOOSS-tahss
MOO-choh tahm-bee-EHN.*

I like you a lot.
Me gustas mucho.
meh GOOSS-tahss MOO-choh.

You're (very) ... .
Eres (muy) ... .
EH-rehss (mwee) ... .

nice [simpático / simpática] *[seem-PAH-tee-koh / seem-PAH-tee-kah]*	**funny** [gracioso / graciosa] *[grah-thee-OH-soh / grah-thee-OH-sah]*	**considerate** [considerado / considerada] *[kohn-see-dheh-RAH-dhoh / kohn-see-dheh-RAH-dhah]*
sweet dulce *DOOL-theh*	**romantic** [romántico / romántica] *[roh-MAHN-tee-koh / roh-MAHN-tee-kah]*	**feminine** femenina *feh-meh-NEE-nah*
tender [tierno / tierna] *[tee-EHR-noh / tee-EHR-nah]*	**[sensual / sensuous]** sensual *sehn-SWAHL*	**manly** hombre *OHM-breh*
interesting interesante *een-teh-reh-SAHN-teh*	**sensitive** sensible *sehn-SEE-bleh*	**beautiful** [bello / bella] *[BEH-yoh / BEH-yah]*
smart inteligente *een-teh-lee-HEHN-teh*	**understanding** [comprensivo / comprensiva] *[kohm-prehn-SEE-voh / kohm-prehn-SEE-vah]*	**goodlooking** [guapo / guapa] *[GWAH-poh / GWAH-pah]*

Mutual Admiration Society

attractive [atractivo / atractiva] *[ah-trahk-TEE-voh / ah-trahk-TEE-vah]*	**[sexy / hot]** sexy *SEHK-see*	**petite** pequeña *peh-KEH-nyah*
	muscular [musculoso / musculosa] *[mooss-koo-LOH-soh / mooss-koo-LOH-sah]*	**slim** [delgado / delgada] *[dehl-GAH-dhoh / dehl-GAH-dhah]*
pretty bonita *boh-NEE-tah*		
cute [mono / mona] *[MOH-noh / MOH-nah]*	**tall** [alto / alta] *[AHL-toh / AHL-tah]*	**curvaceous** voluptuosa *voh-loop-too-OH-sah*
elegant elegante *eh-leh-GAHN-teh*	**big** grande *GRAHN-deh*	**hairy** peludo *peh-LOO-dhoh*

You're great.
Eres [estupendo / estupenda].
*EH-rehss [ehss-too-PEHN-doh /
ehss-too-PEHN-dah].*

You're a good person.
Eres una buena persona.
*EH-rehss OO-nah BWEH-nah
pehr-SOH-nah.*

You're so much fun.
Eres muy [divertido / divertida].
*EH-rehss mwee [dhee-vehr-
TEE-dhoh / dhee-vehr-TEE-dhah].*

You're so stylish.
Siempre estás a la moda.
*see-EHM-preh ehss-TAHSS ah
lah MOH-dhah.*

You're so classy.
Tienes mucha clase.
*tee-EH-nehss MOO-chah
KLAH-seh.*

You're such a gentleman.
Eres un caballero.
EH-rehss oon kah-bah-YEH-roh.

You're so special.
Eres singular.
EH-rehss seen-goo-LAHR.

(Thanks,) you too.
(Gracias,) tú también.
*(GRAH-thee-ahss,) too
tahm-bee-EHN.*

Mutual Admiration Society

I love your ... .
Me encanta tu ... .
meh ehn-KAHN-tah too ... .

personality personalidad *pehr-soh-nah-lee-DHADH*	**clothes** ropa *RROH-pah*	**chin** barbilla *bahr-BEE-yah*	**[navel / belly button]** ombligo *ohm-BLEE-goh*
mind intelecto *een-teh-LEHK-toh*	**earring** pendiente *pehn-dee-EHN-teh*	**mustache** bigote *bee-GOH-teh*	**rear end** trasero *trah-SEH-roh*
style forma de ser *FOHR-mah dheh sehr*	**tattoo** tatuaje *tah-TWAH-heh*	**beard** barba *BAHR-bah*	**ass** culo *KOO-loh*
sense of humor sentido del humor *sehn-TEE-dhoh dhehl oo-MOHR*	**face** cara *KAH-rah*	**neck** cuello *KWEH-yoh*	**vagina** vagina *vah-HEE-nah*
smile sonrisa *sohn-RREE-sah*	**hair** pelo *PEH-loh*	**chest** pecho *PEH-choh*	**pussy** chocho *CHOH-choh*
body cuerpo *KWEHR-poh*	**nose** nariz *nah-REETH*	**torso** torso *TOHR-soh*	**penis** pene *PEH-neh*
figure figura *fee-GOO-rah*	**mouth** boca *BOH-kah*	**back** espalda *ehss-PAHL-dah*	**cock** polla *POH-yah*
tan bronceado *brohn-theh-AH-dhoh*	**tongue** lengua *LEHN-gwah*	**abs** vientre *vee-EHN-treh*	**[basket / bulge]** paquete *pah-KEH-teh*

Mutual Admiration Society

I love your ... .
Me encantan tus ... .
meh ehn-KAHN-tahn tooss ... .

eyes ojos *OH-hohss*	**arms** brazos *BRAH-thohss*	**fingers** dedos *DEH-dhohss*	**pecs** pectorales *pehk-toh-RAH-lehss*
eyebrows cejas *THEH-hahss*	**biceps** bíceps *BEE-thepss*	**nails** uñas *OO-nyahss*	**tits** tetas *TEH-tahss*
eyelashes pestañas *pehss-TAH-nyahss*	**muscles** músculos *MOOSS-koo-lohss*	**curves** curvas *KOOR-vahss*	**buns** nalgas *NAHL-gahss*

I love your toes.
Me encantan los dedos de tus pies.
meh ehn-KAHN-tahn lohss DEH-dhohss deh tooss pee-EHSS.

cheeks *(face)* mejillas *meh-HEE-yahss*			**balls** huevos *WEH-vohss*
dimples hoyuelos *oh-yoo-EH-lohss*			**legs** piernas *pee-EHR-nahss*
lips labios *LAH-bee-ohss*			**thighs** muslos *MOOSS-lohss*
ears orejas *oh-REH-hahss*			**calves** pantorrillas *pahn-toh-RREE-yahss*
earrings pendientes *pehn-dee-EHN-tehss*	**hands** manos *MAH-nohss*	**breasts** pechos *PEH-chohss*	**feet** pies *pee-EHSS*

Mutual Admiration Society ♥ Sexual Ratings

You have a great body.
Tienes un cuerpo estupendo.
*tee-EH-nehss oon KWEHR-poh
ehss-too-PEHN-doh.*

Thanks. You too.
Gracias. Tú también.
*GRAH-thee-ahss. too
tahm-bee-EHN.*

You breasts are so beautiful.
Tienes un pecho muy hermoso.
*tee-EH-nehss oon PEH-choh
mwee ehr-MOH-soh.*

You have such a big cock.
Qué polla más grande tienes.
*keh POH-yah mahss GRAHN-deh
tee-EH-nehss.*

SEXUAL RATINGS

You're great in bed.
Eres [fabuloso / fabulosa] en
la cama.
*EH-rehss [fah-boo-LOH-soh /
fah-boo-LOH-sah] ehn lah
KAH-mah.*

You're a good fuck.
Follas bien.
FOH-yahss bee-EHN.

You're the best.
Eres [el / la] mejor.
EH-rehss [ehl / lah] meh-HOHR.

What a great lover you are.
Qué bien haces el amor.
*keh bee-EHN AH-thehss ehl
ah-MOHR.*

That was great.
Fue genial.
fweh heh-nee-AHL.

! ¡ !

That was so intense.
Fue muy fuerte.
fweh mwee FWEHR-teh.

That was unbelievable.
Fue increíble.
fweh een-kreh-EE-bleh.

**That was the best sex I've ever
had.**
Ha sido el mejor revolcón de mi
vida.
*ah SEE-dhoh ehl meh-HOHR
rreh-vohl-KOHN deh mee
VEE-dhah.*

Love (& War)

I LOVE YOU, I LOVE YOU

I like you (very much).
Me gustas (mucho).
meh GOOSS-tahss (MOO-choh).

I love you (so much)!
¡Te quiero (tanto)!
teh kee-EH-roh (TAHN-toh)!

I'm so in love with you.
Estoy muy [enamorado / enamorada] de ti.
ehss-TOH-ee mwee [eh-nah-moh-RAH-dhoh / eh-nah-moh-RAH-dhah] dheh tee.

I adore you.
Te adoro.
teh ah-DHOH-roh.

I [want / desire] you.
Te deseo.
teh dheh-SEH-oh.

I need you.
Te necesito.
teh neh-theh-SEE-toh.

You are wonderful.
Eres [maravilloso / maravillosa].
EH-rehss [mah-rah-vee-YOH-soh / mah-rah-vee-YOH-sah].

You make me (so) happy.
Me haces (muy) feliz.
meh AH-thehss (mwee) feh-LEETH.

You're the only [man / woman] for me.
Eres [el único hombre / la única mujer] en mi vida.
EH-rehss [ehl OO-nee-koh OHM-breh / lah OO-nee-kah moo-HEHR] ehn mee VEE-dhah.

I can't live without you.
No puedo vivir sin ti.
noh PWEH-dhoh vee-VEER seen tee.

I'm crazy about you.
Estoy [loco / loca] por ti.
ehss-TOH-ee [LOH-koh / LOH-kah] pohr tee.

I can't get you out of my mind.
No puedo olvidarte.
noh PWEH-dhoh ohl-vee-DHAHR-teh.

I Love You, I Love You ♥ Terms of Endearment

I've never felt this way before.
Nunca me he sentido así.
NOON-kah meh eh sehn-TEE-dhoh ah-SEE.

I want to spend the rest of my life with you.
Quiero pasar el resto de mi vida contigo.
kee-EH-roh pah-SAHR ehl RREHSS-toh dheh mee VEE-dhah kohn-TEE-goh.

I've fallen in love with you.
Me he enamorado de ti.
meh eh eh-nah-moh-RAH-dhoh dheh tee.

I'm falling in love with you.
Me estoy enamorando de ti.
meh ehss-TOH-ee eh-nah-moh-RAHN-doh dheh tee.

I am, too.
Yo también.
yoh tahm-bee-EHN.

(Please) don't fall in love with me.
(Por favor) no te enamores de mí.
(pohr fah-VOHR) noh teh eh-nah-MOH-rehss deh mee.

SEE ALSO *LOVE ON THE ROCKS*, NEXT PAGE.

TERMS OF ENDEARMENT

Babe. *(to a girl)*
[Nena *(Sp.)* / Mami *(L.A.)*].
[NEH-nah / MAH-mee].

Babe. *(to a guy)*
[Nene *(Sp.)* / Papi *(L.A.)*].
[NEH-neh / PAH-pee].

(My) baby.
(Mi) [niño / niña].
(mee) [NEE-nyoh / NEE-nyah].

(My) honey.
(Mi) cariño.
(mee) kah-REE-nyoh.

(My) dear.
(Mi) cariño.
(mee) kah-REE-nyoh.

(My) darling.
(Mi) [querido / querida].
(mee) [keh-REE-dhoh / keh-REE-dhah].

(My) love.
(Mi) amor.
(mee) ah-MOHR.

Terms of Endearment ♥ Love on the Rocks

(My) sweetheart.
(Mi) corazón. *(L.A.)*
(mee) koh-rah-THOHN.

(My) doll.
(Mi) [muñeco / muñeca].
*(mee) [moo-NYEH-koh /
moo-NYEH-kah].*

(My) [tiger / tigress].
(Mi) [tigre / tigresa].
(mee) [TEE-greh / tee-GREH-sah].

(My) "pup."
(Mi) [cachorro / cachorra].
*(mee) [kah-CHOH-rroh /
kah-CHOH-rrah].*

LOVE ON THE ROCKS

What's wrong?
¿Qué pasa?
keh PAH-sah?

Is there a problem?
¿Hay algún problema?
AH-ee ahl-GOON proh-BLEH-mah?

Don't you like me anymore?
¿Ya no te gusto?
yah noh teh GOOSS-toh?

It's not that.
No es eso.
noh ehss EH-soh.

I don't like you anymore.
Ya no me gustas.
yah noh meh GOOSS-tahss.

Don't you love me?
¿No me quieres?
noh meh kee-EH-rehss?

I don't love you.
No te quiero.
noh teh kee-EH-roh.

Why don't you love me?
¿Porqué no me quieres?
*pohr-KEH noh meh
kee-EH-rehss?*

I never (really) loved you.
(En realidad) nunca te quise.
*(ehn rreh-ah-lee-DHADH)
NOON-kah teh KEE-seh.*

Love on the Rocks

I like you (a lot), but ... .
Me gustas (mucho), pero ... .
*meh GOOSS-tahss (MOO-choh),
PEH-roh ... .*

---

this isn't working
esto no funciona
EHSS-toh noh foon-thee-OH-nah

you're not the one for me
no eres persona para mí
*noh EH-rehss pehr-SOH-nah
PAH-rah mee*

I'm not in love with you
no estoy [enamorado / enamorada]
de ti
*noh ehss-TOH-ee [eh-nah-moh-
RAH-dhoh / eh-nah-moh-RAH-dhah]
dheh tee*

We don't have much in common.
Tenemos muy poco en común.
*teh-NEH-mohss mwee POH-koh
ehn koh-MOON*

I never promised you anything.
Nunca te prometí nada.
*NOON-kah teh proh-meh-TEE
NAH-dhah.*

**I'm not into a permanent
relationship.**
No quiero una relación seria.
*noh kee-EH-roh OO-nah
rreh-lah-thee-OHN SEH-ree-ah.*

I can't leave my ... .
No puedo dejar a ... .
*noh PWEH-dhoh dheh-HAHR
ah ... .*

[girlfriend / boyfriend]	[wife / husband]	[children / mother]
mi [novia / novio]	mi [mujer / marido]	[mis hijos / mi madre]
mee [NOH-vee-ah / NOH-vee-oh]	*mee [moo-HEHR / mah-REE-dhoh]*	*[meess EE-hohss / mee MAH-dhreh]*

**[He / She] [suspects / found
out] about us.**
[Él / Ella] [sospecha / se enteró]
de lo nuestro.
*[ehl / EH-yah] [sohss-PEH-chah /
seh ehn-teh-ROH] dheh loh
NWEHSS-troh.*

[He / She] is very jealous.
[Él / Ella] es muy [celoso / celosa].
*[ehl / EH-yah] ehss mwee
[theh-LOH-soh / theh-LOH-sah].*

I'm (very) jealous.
Soy (muy) [celoso / celosa].
*SOH-ee (mwee) [theh-LOH-soh /
theh-LOH-sah].*

Don't be so jealous.
No seas tan [celoso / celosa].
*noh SEH-ahss tahn [theh-LOH-
soh / theh-LOH-sah].*

LOVE (& WAR) 83

Love on the Rocks

I'm mad at you.
Estoy [enfadado / enfadada]
contigo.
*ehss-TOH-ee [ehn-fah-DHAH-
dhoh / ehn-fah-DHAH-dhah]
kohn-TEE-goh.*

Don't be mad at me.
No te enfades conmigo.
*noh teh ehn-FAH-dhehss kohn-
MEE-goh.*

You're cheating on me.
Me estás poniendo los cuernos.
*meh ehss-TAHSS poh-nee-EHN-
doh lohss KWEHR-nohss.*

**You betrayed me (with another
[man / woman]).**
Me has traicionado (con [otro
hombre / otra mujer]).
*me ahss trah-ee-thee-oh-NAH-
dhoh (kohn [OH-troh OHM-breh
/ OH-trah moo-HEHR]).*

That's not true.
No es verdad.
noh ehss vehr-DHAHDH.

You're lying.
Estás mintiendo.
ehss-TAHSS meen-tee-EHN-doh.

Don't lie to me.
No me mientas.
noh meh mee-EHN-tahss.

I'm not lying.
No te miento.
noh teh mee-EHN-toh.

Don't give me that crap.
No me vengas con cuentos.
*noh meh VEHN-gahss kohn
KWEHN-tohss.*

You don't own me.
No eres mi [dueño / dueña].
*noh EH-rehss mee [DHWEH-
nyoh / DHWEH-nyah].*

I don't owe you anything.
No te debo nada.
noh teh DHEH-boh NAH-dhah.

Calm down.
Cálmate.
KAHL-mah-teh.

You're manipulating me.
Me estás manipulando.
*meh ehss-TAHSS mah-nee-poo-
LAHN-doh.*

You used me.
Me has utilizado.
meh ahss oo-tee-lee-THAH-dhoh.

Love on the Rocks

You're using me.
Me estás utilizando.
meh ehss-TAHSS oo-tee-lee-THAHN-doh.

You abused me.
Has abusado de mí.
ahss ah-boo-SAH-dhoh dheh mee.

You're abusing me.
Estás abusando de mí.
ehss-TAHSS ah-boo-SAHN-doh dheh mee.

You just want me for [sex / my body / my money].
Me quieres sólo [para follar / por mi cuerpo / por mi dinero].
meh kee-EH-rehss SOH-loh [PAH-rah foh-YAHR / pohr mee KWEHR-poh / pohr mee dhee-NEH-roh].

You don't respect my [feelings / rights / wishes].
No respetas mis [sentimientos / derechos / deseos].
noh rrehss-PEH-tahss meess [sehn-tee-mee-EHN-tohss / deh-REH-chohss / deh-SEH-ohss].

You're so inconsiderate.
Eres [un desconsiderado / una desconsiderada].
EH-rehss [oon dehss-kohn-see-dheh-RAH-dhoh / OO-nah dehss-kohn-see-dheh-RAH-dhah].

You're always full of excuses.
Tienes excusas para todo.
tee-EH-nehss ehks-KOO-sahss PAH-rah TOH-dhoh.

Be reasonable.
Sé razonable.
seh rrah-thoh-NAH-bleh.

I want us to stay friends.
Quiero que seamos amigos.
kee-EH-roh keh seh-AH-mohss ah-MEE-gohss.

I'm sorry. It's over.
Lo siento. Se acabó.
loh see-EHN-toh. seh ah-kah-BOH.

You don't want to see me again?
¿No me quieres volver a ver?
noh meh kee-EH-rehss vohl-VEHR ah vehr?

Love on the Rocks ♥ Insults, Part I

We can still see each other.
Nos podemos ver.
nohss poh-DHEH-mohss VEHR.

But not right away.
Pero no enseguida.
PEH-roh noh ehn-seh-GHEE-dhah.

I don't want to see you again.
No te quiero volver a ver.
noh teh kee-EH-roh vohl-VEHR ah vehr.

How can you say that?
¿Cómo puedes decirme eso?
KOH-moh PWEH-dhehss dheh-THEER-meh EH-soh?

You've gone too far.
Te has pasado.
teh ahss pah-SAH-dhoh.

I'm sorry I ever met you.
Lamento haberte conocido.
lah-MEHN-toh ah-BEHR-teh koh-noh-THEE-dhoh.

INSULTS, PART I

Damn you!
¡Vete al cuerno!
VEH-teh ahl KWEHR-noh!

Go to hell!
¡Vete al infierno!
VEH-teh ahl een-fee-EHR-noh!

Drop dead!
¡Mal rayo te parta!
mahl RRAH-yoh teh PAHR-tah!

Kiss my ass!
¡Me cago en tu estampa!
meh KAH-goh ehn too ehss-TAHM-pah!

Fuck! *(gen. exclamation)*
¡Coño!
KOH-nyoh!

Fuck you!
¡Vete a tomar por culo!
VEH-teh ah toh-MAHR pohr KOO-loh!

I hate you.
Te odio.
teh OH-dhee-oh.

INSULTS, PART II

Here's everything you need to let him or her "have it." Like in English, you don't always have to say "You're a..."; your insult can stand defiantly alone. Take a noun by itself from the left column—or if that's not enough, add an adjective from the right column (Spanish adjectives usually come *after* the noun). Adjectives can also work as nouns by themselves; it's fine to say "You're a..." plus an adjective.

But remember: Once you say it, it's not always easy to take back, so watch out with these words!

(You're a ... .)   **(Don't be a ... .)**
(Eres [un / una] ... .)   (No seas ... .)
(EH-rehss [oon / OO-nah] ... .)   *(noh SEH-ahss ... .)*

NOUNS	ADJECTIVES
jerk *(man or woman)* gilipollas *hee-lee-POH-yahss*	**stupid** [estúpido / estúpida] *[ehss-TOO-pee-dhoh / ehs-TOO-pee-dhah]*
prick *(men only)* mamón *mah-MOHN*	**fucked-up** [jodido / jodida] *[hoh-DHEE-dhoh / hoh-DHEE-dhah]*
dick *(men only)* capullo *kah-POO-yoh*	**crazy** [loco / loca] *[LOH-koh / LOH-kah]*
asshole [cabrón / cabrona] *[kah-BROHN / kah-BROH-nah]*	**sleazy** [vicioso / viciosa] *[vee-thee-OH-soh / vee-thee-OH-sah]*

NOUNS

bastard
borde
BOHR-deh

[son-of-a-bitch / bitch]
[hijo / hija] de puta
[EE-hoh / EE-hah] dheh POO-tah

whore
puta
POO-tah

slut
pendón
pen-DOHN

sadist
[sádico / sádica]
[SAH-dhee-koh / SAH-dhee-kah]

psycho
psicópata
see-KOH-pah-tah

idiot
idiota
ee-dhee-OH-tah

golddigger
[interesado / interesada]
*[een-teh-reh-SAH-dhoh /
een-teh-reh-SAH-dhah]*

sleaze
[vicioso / viciosa]
[vee-thee-OH-soh / vee-thee-OH-sah]

hypocrite
hipócrita
ee-POH-kree-tah

ADJECTIVES

filthy
[guarro / guarra]
[GWAH-rroh / GWAH-rrah]

shitty
de mierda
deh mee-EHR-dah

disgusting
[asqueroso / asquerosa]
[ahss-keh-ROH-soh / ahss-keh-ROH-sah]

[unfeeling / insensitive]
insensible
een-sehn-SEE-bleh

heartless
[inhumano / inhumana]
[een-oo-MAH-noh / een-oo-MAH-nah]

cruel
cruel
kroo-EHL

nasty
desagradable
deh-sah-grah-DHAH-bleh

lying
[mentiroso / mentirosa]
[mehn-tee-ROH-soh / mehn-tee-ROH-sah]

[two-faced / hypocritical]
hipócrita
ee-POH-kree-tah

scheming
intrigante
een-tree-GAHN-teh

Insults, Part II

NOUNS	ADJECTIVES
liar [mentiroso / mentirosa] *[mehn-tee-ROH-soh / mehn-tee-ROH-sah]*	**bossy** [mandón / mandona] *[mahn-DOHN / mahn-DOH-nah]*
creep [retorcido / retorcida] *[rreh-tohr-THEE-dhoh /* *rreh-tohr-THEE-dhah]*	**possessive** [posesivo / posesiva] *[poh-seh-SEE-voh / poh-seh-SEE-vah]*
brute burro *BOO-rroh*	**manipulating** [manipulador / manipuladora] *[mah-nee-poo-lah-DHOHR /* *mah-nee-poo-lah-DHOH-rah]*
monster monstruo *(male or female)* *MOHNSS-troo-oh*	**backstabbing** [traidor / traidora] *[trah-ee-DHOHR / trah-ee-DHOH-rah]*
cheapskate [agarrado / agarrada] *[ah-gah-RRAH-dhoh / ah-gah-RRAH-dhah]*	**evil-minded** [malpensado / malpensada] *[mahl-pehn-SAH-dhoh /* *mahl-pehn-SAH-dhah]*
coward cobarde *koh-BAHR-deh*	**money-hungry** [avaricioso / avariciosa] *[ah-vah-ree-thee-OH-soh /* *ah-vah-ree-thee-OH-sah]*
swine canalla *kah-NAH-yah*	**cheap** [tacaño / tacaña] *[tah-KAH-nyoh / tah-KAH-nyah]*
leech sanguijuela *sahn-ghee-HWEH-lah*	**ungrateful** [ingrato / ingrata] *[een-GRAH-toh / een-GRAH-tah]*
pig [cerdo / cerda] *[THEHR-dhoh / THEHR-dhah]*	**selfish** egoísta *eh-goh-EESS-tah*
rat rata *RRAH-tah*	**hysterical** [histérico / histérica] *[eess-TEH-ree-koh / eess-TEH-ree-kah]*

Don't be a pain in the neck.
No seas [pesado / pesada].
noh SEH-ahss [peh-SAH-dhoh / peh-SAH-dhah].

What a pain you are!
¡Qué [pesado / pesada] eres!
keh [peh-SAH-dhoh / peh-SAH-dhah] EH-rehss!

MAKING UP

I'm sorry.
Lo siento.
loh see-EHN-toh.

You were right.
Tenías razón.
teh-NEE-ahss rrah-THOHN.

I was wrong.
Yo no tenía razón.
yoh noh teh-NEE-ah rrah-THOHN.

We were both wrong.
Los dos no teníamos razón.
lohss dohss noh teh-NEE-ah-mohss rrah-THOHN.

I shouldn't have said that.
No debería haberte dicho eso.
noh dheh-beh-REE-ah ah-BEHR-teh DHEE-choh EH-soh.

I didn't mean what I said.
Lo dije sin querer.
loh DHEE-heh seen keh-REHR.

I always say things I don't mean.
Siempre digo cosas sin querer.
see-EHM-preh DHEE-goh KOH-sahss seen keh-REHR.

It doesn't mean anything.
No quiere decir nada.
noh kee-EH-reh dheh-THEER NAH-dhah.

I never meant to hurt you.
Nunca quise herirte.
NOON-kah KEE-seh eh-REER-teh.

I've had a rough day.
He tenido un día difícil.
eh teh-NEE-dhoh oon DEE-ah dhee-FEE-theel.

Don't be mad at me.
No te enfades conmigo.
noh teh ehn-FAH-dhehss kohn-MEE-goh.

I always screw up relationships.
Siempre jodo las relaciones.
see-EHM-preh HOH-dhoh lahss rreh-lah-thee-OH-nehss.

LOVE (& WAR)

Making Up

I'm terrible.
Soy horrible.
SOH-ee oh-RREE-bleh.

No, you're not.
No lo eres.
noh loh EH-rehss.

I lost control.
Perdí el control.
pehr-DHEE ehl kohn-TROHL.

Let's make up.
Vamos a arreglarnos.
VAH-mohss ah ah-rreh-GLAHR-nohss.

Can we forget it happened?
¿Olvidamos lo que pasó?
ohl-vee-DHAH-mohss loh keh pah-SOH?

Can you forgive me?
¿Me puedes perdonar?
meh PWEH-dhehss pehr-dhoh-NAHR?

I forgive you.
Te perdono.
teh pehr-DHOH-noh.

I can't forgive you.
No te puedo perdonar.
noh teh PWEH-dhoh pehr-dhoh-NAHR.

Give me [another / one last] chance.
Dame [otra / una última] oportunidad.
DAH-meh [OH-trah / OO-nah OOL-tee-mah] oh-pohr-too-nee-DHADH.

This [is / was] your last chance.
Ésta [va a ser / fue] la última oportunidad.
EHSS-tah [vah ah sehr / fweh] lah OOL-tee-mah oh-pohr-too-nee-DHADH.

I still love you.
Todavía te quiero.
toh-dhah-VEE-ah teh kee-EH-roh.

I'll never hurt you again.
No te heriré nunca más.
noh teh eh-ree-REH NOON-kah mahss.

Can we try again?
¿Podemos empezar de nuevo?
poh-DHEH-mohss ehm-peh-THAHR dheh NWEH-voh?

Let's start over.
Vamos a empezar de nuevo.
VAH-mohss ah ehm-peh-THAHR dheh NWEH-voh.

Search for Tomorrow

LIMITS & RULES

What are you looking for?
¿Qué intenciones tienes?
*keh een-tehn-thee-OH-nehss
tee-EH-nehss?*

I don't know.
No lo sé.
noh loh seh.

I'm looking for ... .
Estoy buscando ... .
ehss-TOH-ee booss-KAHN-doh ... .

love
amor
ah-MOHR

a [husband / wife]
[marido / mujer]
[mah-REE-dhoh / moo-HEHR]

a [boyfriend / girlfriend]
[novio / novia]
[NOH-vee-oh / NOH-vee-ah]

marriage
casarme
kah-SAHR-meh

a long-term relationship
una relación estable
*OO-nah rreh-lah-thee-OHN
ehss-TAH-bleh*

an open relationship
una relación abierta
*OO-nah rreh-lah-thee-OHN
ah-bee-EHR-tah*

(mostly) friendship
(más que nada) amistad
*(mahss keh NAH-dhah)
ah-meess-TADH*

nothing too serious
algo no muy serio
AHL-goh noh mwee SEH-ree-oh

just sex
sólo sexo
SOH-loh SEHK-soh

a good lay
un buen revolcón
oon bwehn rreh-vohl-KOHN

SHACKING UP

I'd like to live with you.
Quisiera vivir contigo.
*kee-see-EH-rah vee-VEER
kohn-TEE-goh.*

Maybe I could stay here.
Quizá pueda quedarme aquí.
*kee-THAH PWEH-dhah
keh-DHAHR-meh
ah-KEE.*

We could live together [here / in my country].
Pudiéramos vivir juntos [aquí / en mi país].
poo-dhee-EH-rah-mohss vee-VEER HOON-tohss [ah-KEE / ehn mee pah-EESS].

I'll teach you English and you can teach me Spanish.
Te enseño inglés y tú me enseñas español.
teh ehn-seh-nyoh een-GLEHSS ee too meh ehn-SEH-nyahss ehss-pah-NYOHL.

I'd like that (a lot).
Me gustaría (mucho).
*meh gooss-tah-REE-ah
(MOO-choh).*

(But) it's too soon.
(Pero) es demasiado pronto.
*(PEH-roh) ehss
deh-mah-see-AH-
dhoh PROHN-toh.*

Let's get to know each other better.
Vamos a esperar a conocernos mejor.
*VAH-mohss ah ehss-peh-RAHR
ah koh-noh-THEHR-nohss
meh-HOHR.*

I'll come visit you (as soon as possible).
Vendré a visitarte (lo más pronto posible).
*vehn-DREH ah vee-see-TAHR-teh
(loh mahss PROHN-toh
poh-SEE-bleh).*

Then we'll see.
Ya veremos qué pasa.
*yah veh-REH-mohss keh
PAH-sah.*

WEDDING BELLS

Would you marry me?
¿Te casarías conmigo?
teh kah-sah-REE-ahss kohn-MEE-goh?

Let's get married.
Vamos a casarnos.
VAH-mohss ah kah-SAHR-nohss.

I'd love to.
Me encantaría.
meh ehn-kahn-tah-REE-ah.

I want a [church / civil] wedding.
Quiero una boda [en la iglesia / civil].
kee-EH-roh OO-nah BOH-dhah [ehn lah ee-GLEH-see-ah / thee-VEEL].

Let's elope.
Vamos a fugarnos.
VAH-mohss ah foo-GAHR-nohss.

(I like you very much, but) ... .
(Me gustas mucho, pero) ... .
(meh GOOSS-tahss MOO-choh, PEH-roh) ... .

I can't
no puedo
noh PWEH-dhoh

it's too soon
es demasiado pronto
ehss deh-mah-see-AH-dhoh PROHN-toh

the time's not right
no es el momento
noh ehss ehl moh-MEHN-toh

we don't know each other well enough
no nos conocemos bastante bien
noh nohss koh-noh-THEH-mohss bahss-TAHN-teh bee-EHN

I need to think it over
necesito pensarlo
neh-theh-SEE-toh pehn-SAHR-loh

my life is too complicated right now
mi vida es muy complicada en este momento
mee VEE-dhah ehss mwee kohm-plee-KAH-dhah ehn EHSS-teh moh-MEHN-toh

I'm not in love with you
no estoy [enamorado / enamorada] de ti
noh ehss-TOH-ee [eh-nah-moh-RAH-dhoh / eh-nah-moh-RAH-dhah] dheh tee

SEE ALSO *LOVE ON THE ROCKS* (P. 81).

Goodbye Time

I've had a great time with you.
Me lo he pasado muy bien contigo.
*meh loh eh pah-SAH-dhoh
mwee bee-EHN kohn-TEE-goh.*

I wish I didn't have to leave.
Ojalá no tuviera que irme.
*oh-hah-LAH noh too-vee-EH-rah
keh EER-meh.*

(Please) don't leave.
(Por favor) no te marches.
*(pohr fah-VOHR) noh teh
MAHR-chehss.*

**Don't leave
me.**
No me dejes.
*noh meh
DHEH-hehss.*

Don't cry.
No llores.
noh YOH-rehss.

Will you miss me?
¿Me echarás de
menos?
*meh eh-chah-RAHSS deh
MEH-nohss?*

I'll miss you (so much).
Te echaré (mucho) de menos.
*teh eh-chah-REH (MOO-choh)
dheh MEH-nohss.*

Come visit me.
Ven a verme.
vehn ah VEHR-meh.

When will you visit me?
¿Cuándo vendrás a verme?
*KWAHN-doh vehn-DRAHSS
ah VEHR-meh?*

I'll visit you (soon).
Te vendré a visitar (pronto).
*teh vehn-DREH ah vee-
see-TAHR (PROHN-toh).*

SEE ALSO APPENDIX A: *WHEN?*
(P. 105) AND *MONTHLY
MINDER* (P. 109).

**Let's write each
other.**
Vamos a escribirnos.
*VAH-mohss ah ehss-kree-
BEER-nohss.*

**We can talk on the phone
(every week).**
Podemos llamarnos (todas las
semanas).
*poh-DHEH-mohss yah-MAHR-
nohss (TOH-dhahss lahss
seh-MAH-nahss).*

SEE ALSO APPENDIX A: *WHEN?* (P. 105).

(Please) don't see anyone (while I'm gone).
(Por favor) no salgas con nadie (mientras estoy fuera).
(pohr fah-VOHR) noh SAHL-gahss kohn NAH-dhee-eh (mee-EHN-trahss ehss-TOH-ee FWEH-rah).

You can go out with other people.
Puedes salir con otra gente.
PWEH-dhehss sah-LEER kohn OH-trah HEHN-teh.

One last [hug / kiss].
Dame el último [abrazo / beso].
DAH-meh ehl OOL-tee-moh [ah-BRAH-thoh / BEH-soh].

Could you come with me to the ... ?
¿Me puedes acompañar ... ?
meh PWEH-dhehss ah-kohm-pah-NYAHR ... ?

---

airport
al aeropuerto
ahl ah-eh-roh-PWEHR-toh

(train) station
a la estación (de trenes)
ah lah ehss-tah-thee-OHN (deh TREH-nehss)

bus station
a la estación de autobuses
ah lah ehss-tah-thee-OHN deh ah-oo-toh-BOO-sehss

Better not.
Mejor que no.
meh-HOHR keh noh.

I don't like goodbyes.
No me gustan las despedidas.
noh meh GOOSS-tahn lahss dehss-peh-DHEE-dhahss.

Let's say goodbye here.
Vamos a despedirnos aquí.
VAH-mohss ah dhehss-peh-DHEER-nohss ah-KEE.

Take care.
Cuídate.
KWEE-dhah-teh.

Don't forget about me.
No me olvides.
noh meh ohl-VEE-dhehss.

I won't (ever) forget you.
No te olvidaré (jamás).
noh teh ohl-vee-dhah-REH (hah-MAHSS).

I'll always think about you.
Siempre pensaré en ti.
see-EHM-preh pehn-sah-REH ehn tee.

Shop Talk

JUST LOOKING

Can you help me?
Me puede ayudar?
*meh PWEH-dheh
ah-yoo-DHAHR?*

May I help you?
[Lo / La] puedo ayudar?
*[loh / lah] PWEH-dhoh
ah-yoo-DHAHR?*

I'm just looking, (thank you).
Sólo estoy mirando, (gracias).
*SOH-loh ehss-TOH-ee
mee-RAHN-doh, (GRAH-thee-ahss).*

I'm looking for ... , (please).
(Por favor) estoy buscando ... .
*(pohr fah-VOHR,) ehss-TOH-ee
booss-KAHN-doh ... .*

Do you have ... ?
¿Tiene ... ?
tee-EH-neh ... ?

([engagement / wedding]) rings anillos (de [compromiso / matrimonio]) *ah-NEE-yohss (deh [kohm-proh-MEE-soh / mah-tree-MOH-nee-oh])*	**birth-control pills** píldoras anticonceptivas *PEEL-doh-rahss ahn-tee-kohn-thehp-TEE-vahss*	**[extra-large / female] condoms** condones [grandes / femeninos] *kohn-DOH-nehss [GRAHN-dehss / feh-meh-NEE-nohss]*
spermicidal [foam / cream / gel / sponges]. [espuma / crema / jalea / una esponja] espermicida *[ehss-POO-mah / KREH-mah / hah-LEH-ah / OO-nah ehss-POHN-hah] ehss-pehr-mee-THEE-dhah.*	**a diaphragm** un diafragma *oon dee-ah-FRAHG-mah* **[lubricated / unlubricated] condoms** condones [con / sin] lubricante *kohn-DOH-nehss [kohn / seen] loo-bree-KAHN-teh*	**a (water-soluble) lubricant** un lubricante (hidro-soluble) *oon loo-bree-KAHN-teh (ee-dhroh-soh-LOO-bleh)* **crotchless panties** bragas abiertas *BRAH-gahss ah-bee-EHR-tahss*

bikini panties
bragas de bikini
*BRAH-gahss dheh
bee-KEE-nee*

string panties
bragas de tanga
*BRAH-gahss dheh
TAHN-gah*

a corset
un corsé
oon kohr-SEH

a teddy
un susana
oon soo-SAH-nah

garters
ligueros
lee-GHEH-rohss

**erotic [greeting cards
/ postcards]**
postales eróticas
*pohss-TAH-lehss
eh-ROH-tee-kahss*

**porn [magazines /
videos]**
[revistas / vídeos] porno
*[rreh-VEESS-tahss /
VEE-dheh-ohss]
POHR-noh*

a dildo
un consolador
*oon kohn-soh-lah-
DHOHR*

a vibrator
un vibrador
oon vee-brah-DHOHR

a nipple ring
un pendiente de pezón
*oon pehn-dee-EHN-teh
dheh peh-THOHN*

nipple clips
pinzas para pezones
*PEEN-thahss PAH-rah
peh-THOH-nehss*

handcuffs
esposas
ehss-POH-sahss

chains
cadenas
kah-DHEH-nahss

a harness
un arnés
oon ahr-NEHSS

a (studded) collar
un collar (con clavos)
*oon koh-YAHR (kohn
KLAH-vohss)*

a whip
un látigo
oon LAH-tee-goh

**an inflatable [male /
female] doll**
[un muñeco / una
muñeca] inflable
*[oon moo-NYEH-koh /
OO-nah moo-NYEH-
kah] een-FLAH-bleh*

MORE INFO

How much does this cost?
¿Cuánto vale esto?
KWAHN-toh VAH-leh EHSS-toh?

SEE *HOW MUCH?* (P. 106).

**(I don't understand.) Can you
write the price down for me?**
(No entiendo.) ¿Me puede
escribir el precio?
*(noh ehn-tee-EHN-doh.) meh
PWEH-dheh ehss-kree-BEER
ehl PREH-thee-oh?*

Are these condoms latex?
¿Son de látex estos condones?
*sohn deh LAH-tehks EHSS-
tohss kohn-DOH-nehss?*

Is this lubricant water-soluble?
¿Es hidrosoluble este lubricante?
*ehss ee-dhroh-soh-LOO-bleh
EHSS-teh loo-bree-KAHN-teh?*

Does it have a spermicide?
¿Contiene espermicida?
*kohn-tee-EH-neh ehss-pehr-mee-
THEE-dhah?*

ADJUSTMENTS

It's not what I'm looking for.
No es lo que busco.
noh ehss loh keh BOOSS-koh.

Do you have another ... ?
¿Tiene ... ?
tee-EH-neh ... ?

size	style	color
otra talla	otro modelo	otro color
OH-trah	*OH-troh*	*OH-troh*
TAH-yah	*moh-DHEH-loh*	*koh-LOHR*

Do you have anything ... ?
¿No tiene algo más ... ?
*noh tee-EH-neh ALH-goh
mahss ... ?*

bigger	softer
grande	suave
GRAHN-deh	*SWAH-veh*
smaller	**better**
pequeño	de calidad
peh-KEH-nyoh	*deh kah-lee-DHADH*
harder	**less expensive**
duro	barato
DOO-roh	*bah-RAH-toh*

Colón

PESO

Peseta

Dólar

bolívar

To Your Health

SWAPPING HISTORIES

Do you sleep around a lot?
¿Te acuestas con mucha gente?
teh ah-KWEHSS-tahss kohn MOO-chah HEHN-teh?

I have (not) slept around a lot.
(No) me he acostado con mucha gente.
(noh) meh eh ah-kohss-TAH-dhoh kohn MOO-chah HEHN-teh.

Have you always had safe sex?
¿Siempre has practicado sexo seguro?
see-EHM-preh ahss prahk-tee-KAH-dhoh SEHK-soh seh-GOO-roh?

I've always had safe sex.
Siempre he practicado sexo seguro.
see-EHM-preh eh prahk-tee-KAH-dhoh SEHK-soh seh-GOO-roh.

I've always used condoms.
Siempre he usado condones.
see-EHM-preh eh oo-SAH-dhoh kohn-DOH-nehss.

I haven't always used condoms.
No siempre he usado condones.
noh see-EHM-preh eh oo-SAH-dhoh kohn-DOH-nehss.

I've started using condoms recently.
Hace poco que uso condones.
AH-theh POH-koh keh OO-soh kohn-DOH-nehss.

Have you been tested for HIV (recently)?
¿Te has hecho la prueba del SIDA (últimamente)?
teh ahss EH-choh lah PRWEH-bah dhehl SEE-dhah (OOL-tee-mah-MEHN-teh)?

I haven't taken the test.
No me he hecho la prueba.
noh meh eh EH-choh lah PRWEH-bah.

I was tested in [March / July].
Me hice la prueba en [marzo / julio].
meh EE-theh lah PRWEH-bah ehn [MAHR-thoh / HOO-lee-oh].

SEE ALSO APPENDIX A: *WHEN?* (P. 105) AND *MONTHLY MINDER* (P. 109).

I am HIV-negative.
Soy [seronegativo / seronegativa].
SOH-ee [seh-roh-neh-gah-TEE-voh / seh-roh-neh-gah-TEE-vah].

I am HIV-positive.
Soy [seropositivo / seropositiva].
SOH-ee [seh-roh-poh-see-TEE-voh / seh-roh-poh-see-TEE-vah].

But I'm healthy.
Pero no tengo síntomas.
PEH-roh noh TEHN-goh SEEN-toh-mahss.

I have AIDS.
Tengo el SIDA.
TEHN-goh ehl SEE-dah.

I was diagnosed [six months / a year / three years] ago.
Me lo diagnosticaron hace [seis meses / un año / tres años].
meh loh dee-ahg-nohss-tee-KAH-rohn AH-theh [SEH-eess MEH-sehss / oon AH-nyoh / trehss AH-nyohss].

SEE ALSO APPENDIX A: *A ONE AND A TWO...* (P. 107).

Have you had any STD's (sexually transmitted diseases)?
¿Has tenido alguna enfermedad venérea?
ahss teh-NEE-dhoh ahl-GOO-nah ehn-fehr-meh-DHADH veh-NEH-reh-ah?

Not that I know of.
Que yo sepa, no.
keh yoh SEH-pah, noh.

I haven't had any venereal diseases.
No he tenido ninguna enfermedad venérea.
noh eh teh-NEE-dhoh neen-GOO-nah ehn-fehr-meh-DHADH veh-NEH-reh-ah.

I've had ... .
He tenido ... .
eh teh-NEE-dhoh ... .

I have ... .
Tengo ... .
TEHN-goh ... .

gonorrhea	hepatitis	chlamydia
gonorrea	hepatitis	clamídeas
goh-noh-RREH-ah	*eh-pah-TEE-teess*	*klah-MEE-dheh-ahss*
syphilis	**herpes**	**[crabs / pubic lice]**
sífilis	herpes	ladillas
SEE-fee-leess	*EHR-pehss*	*lah-DHEE-yahss*

When?
¿Cuando?
KWAHN-doh?

Recently.
Hace poco.
AH-theh POH-koh.

A long time ago.
Hace mucho tiempo.
AH-theh MOO-choh tee-EHM-poh.

SEE ALSO *WHEN?* (P. 105).

We'll be careful, (okay?)
Iremos con cuidado, (¿vale?)
ee-REH-mohss kohn kwee-DHAH-dhoh, (VAH-leh?)

I'm (very) sorry.
Lo siento (mucho).
loh see-EHN-toh (MOO-choh).

(I like you, but) I'd rather not.
(Me gustas, pero) mejor lo dejamos.
(meh GOOSS-tahss, PEH-roh) meh-HOHR loh dheh-HAH-mohss.

(Please) don't be offended.
(Por favor) no te ofendas.
(pohr fah-VOHR,) noh teh oh-FEHN-dahss.

I hope we can be friends.
Espero que podamos ser amigos.
ehss-PEH-roh keh poh-DHAH-mohss sehr ah-MEE-gohss.

=====
1+1=3
=====

Are you pregnant?
¿Estás embarazada?
ehss-TAHSS ehm-bah-rah-THAH-dah?

(I think) I'm pregnant.
(Creo que) estoy embarazada.
(KREH-oh keh) ehss-TOH-ee ehm-bah-rah-THAH-dah.

That's great!
¡Estupendo!
ehss-too-PEHN-doh!

That's a (big) problem.
Eso es un problema (grave).
EH-soh ehss oon proh-BLEH-mah (GRAH-veh).

We're not ready.
No estamos listos.
noh ehss-TAH-mohss LEESS-tohss.

Have you seen a doctor?
¿Has ido al médico?
ahss EE-dhoh ahl MEH-dhee-koh?

Come with me to the doctor.
Ven conmigo al médico.
vehn kohn-MEE-goh ahl MEH-dhee-koh.

Should we have the child?
¿Crees que debamos tenerlo?
KREH-ehss keh dheh-BAH-mohss teh-NEHR-loh?

(Of course) I want the child.
(Claro que) quiero tenerlo.
(KLAH-roh keh) kee-EH-roh teh-NEHR-loh.

I don't want the child.
No lo quiero.
noh loh kee-EH-roh.

Should we give the child up for adoption?
¿Lo damos para adopción?
loh DHAH-mohss PAH-rah ah-dhohp-thee-OHN?

I don't know what to do.
No sé que hacer.
noh seh keh ah-THEHR.

Will you help me?
¿Me vas a ayudar?
meh vahss ah ah-yoo-DHAHR?

I'll help you.
Te voy a ayudar.
teh VOH-ee ah ah-yoo-DHAHR.

SEE ALSO *WEDDING BELLS* (P. 93).

WHAT'S UP, DOC?

I need a doctor.
Necesito un médico.
*neh-theh-SEE-toh oon
MEH-dhee-koh.*

Do you know a good doctor?
¿Conoces un buen médico?
*koh-NOH-thehss oon bwehn
MEH-dhee-koh?*

I need a check-up.
Necesito un examen médico.
*neh-theh-SEE-toh oon ehk-SAH-
mehn MEH-dhee-koh.*

I don't feel well.
No me siento bien.
noh meh see-EHN-toh bee-EHN.

It hurts (here).
Me duele (aquí).
meh DHWEH-leh (ah-KEE).

**I may have caught [... / some-
thing].**
Temo haber contraído [... / algo].
*TEH-moh ah-BEHR kohn-trah-
EE-dhoh [... / AHL-goh].*

FOR NAMES OF SEXUALLY TRANSMITTED
DISEASES, SEE *SWAPPING HISTORIES*
(P. 101).

I'd like to be tested for ... .
Quisiera hacerme la prueba del ... .
*kee-see-EH-rah ah-THEHR-meh
lah PRWEH-bah dhehl... .*

pregnancy	AIDS
embarazo	SIDA
ehm-bah-RAH-thoh	*SEE-dhah*

EMERGENCIES

Help!
¡Socorro!
soh-KOH-rroh!

I need the police.
Llame a la policia.
YAH-meh ah lah poh-lee-THEE-ah.

(Please) take me to a hospital.
(Por favor) lléveme a un hospital.
*(pohr fah-VOHR,) YEH-veh-meh
ah oon ohss-pee-TAHL.*

I've been robbed.
Me han robado.
meh ahn rroh-BAH-dhoh.

I've been beaten.
Me han pegado.
meh ahn peh-GAH-dhoh.

I've been raped.
Me han violado.
meh ahn vee-oh-LAH-dhoh.

Appendix A: Handy Little Words

SHORT & SWEET	WHO?

SHORT & SWEET

and
y *(changes to "e" before words beginning with "i")*

or
o *(changes to "u" before words beginning with "o")*

with
con

without
sin

[good / well]
[bueno / bien]

[better / the best]
[mejor / el mejor]

[bad / badly]
[malo / mal]

[worse / the worst]
[peor / el peor]

so-so
regular

WHO?

Who?
¿Quién?

I
Yo

You *(inf.)*
Tú

You *(formal)*
Usted

He
Él

She
Ella

We
[Nosotros / Nosotras]

You *(inf. pl. in Sp. but not L.A.)*
[Vosotros / Vosotras]

You *(formal pl. in Sp.; gen. pl. in L.A.)*
Ustedes

They *(male or mixed)*
Ellos

They *(female)*
Ellas

That one *(male)*
Aquél

That one *(female)*
Aquélla

WHAT?

What?
¿Qué?

This
Esto

That
Eso

That over there
Aquello

WHEN?

When?
¿Cuándo?

Now
Ahora

Soon
Pronto

Today
Hoy

Yesterday
Ayer

The day before yesterday
Anteayer

Tomorrow
Mañana

The day after tomorrow
Pasado mañana

On [Friday / Sunday]
El [viernes / domingo]

SEE ALSO *IF IT'S TUESDAY...* (P. 109).

This [week / weekend].
[Esta semana / Este fin de semana].

Last [week / month / year]
[La semana pasada / El mes pasado / El año pasado]

Next [week / month / year]
[La semana / El mes / El año] que viene

In a few [weeks / months / years]
Dentro de [unas semanas / unos meses / unos años]

In [May / December]
En [mayo / diciembre]

SEE ALSO *MONTHLY MINDER* (P. 109).

Always
Siempre

Sometimes
A veces

Never
Jamás

WHERE?

Where?
¿Dónde?

Where to?
¿Adónde?

Here
Aquí

There
[Allí / Ahí]

On the left
A la izquierda

On the right
A la derecha

[In the back / Behind]
Detrás

In front
Delante

On the side (of ...)
Al lado (de ...)

[Upstairs / On top / Above]
Arriba

[Downstairs / On the bottom / Below]
Abajo

Outside
Fuera

Inside
Dentro

WHY?

Why?
¿Por qué?

Why not?
¿Por qué no?

Because ...
Porque ...

HOW MUCH?

How much?
¿Cuánto?

[One hundred fifty / five hundred] pesetas
[Ciento cincuenta / quinientas] pesetas*

* A SLANG WORD FOR PESETAS, SPAIN'S CURRENCY, IS *PELAS*—LIKE SAYING "BUCKS" FOR DOLLARS.

A ONE AND A TWO...

one uno	**eleven** once	**twenty-one** veintiuno	**one hundred** cien
two dos	**twelve** doce	**twenty-two** veintidós	**one hundred ten** ciento diez
three tres	**thirteen** trece	**thirty** treinta	**two hundred** doscientos (/-as)
four cuatro	**fourteen** catorce	**forty** cuarenta	**five hundred** quinientos (/-as)
five cinco	**fifteen** quince	**fifty** cincuenta	**five hundred fifty** quinientos (/-as) cincuenta
six seis	**sixteen** dieciséis	**sixty** sesenta	**one thousand** mil
seven siete	**seventeen** diecisiete	**seventy** setenta	**two thousand** dos mil
eight ocho	**eighteen** dieciocho	**eighty** ochenta	**two thousand five hundred** dos mil quinientos (/-as)
nine nueve	**nineteen** diecinueve	**ninety** noventa	**five thousand** cinco mil
ten diez	**twenty** veinte	**ninety-nine** noventa y nueve	

CLOCKWISE

A FEW EXAMPLES FOR TELLING TIME:

It's 8 P.M.
Son las ocho.

It's 20:00.
Son las veinte
horas.

SOMETIMES EURO-
PEANS AND LATIN
AMERICANS USE THE 24-
HOUR CLOCK; INSTEAD OF
8 P.M., THEY'LL SAY
"20:00" (THE TWENTIETH
HOUR OF THE DAY).

At 8:05.
A las ocho y cinco. *("eight and five")*

By 8:15.
Antes de las ocho y quince. *("eight and fifteen")*

It's quarter after eight.
Son las ocho y cuarto. *("eight and quarter")*

After 8:30.
Después de las ocho y media. *("eight and half")*

Around 8:40.
Cerca de las ocho y cuarenta. *("eight and forty")*

> **It's twenty to nine.**
> Son las nueve menos veinte. *("nine minus twenty")*

> **It's 8:45.**
> Son las ocho y cuarenta y cinco. *("eight and forty-five")*

> **It's quarter to nine.**
> Son las nueve menos cuarto. *("nine minus quarter")*

> **In the morning.**
> De la mañana.

In the afternoon.
De la tarde.

In the evening.
De la tarde.

At night.
De la noche.

At midnight.
A medianoche.

At noon.
A mediodía.

IF IT'S TUESDAY...

Today is ... .
Hoy es ... .

Tomorrow is ... .
Mañana es ... .

Next ... .
El próximo ... .

Last ... .
El ... pasado.

(On) ... morning.
El ... por la mañana.

(On) ... afternoon.
El ... por la tarde.

(On) ... evening.
El ... por la tarde.

(On) ... night.
El ... por la noche.

Monday	lunes
Tuesday	martes
Wednesday	miércoles
Thursday	jueves
Friday	viernes
Saturday	sábado
Sunday	domingo

MONTHLY MINDER

[It's / We're in] ... .
Estamos en ... .

[In / Last / Next] ... .
En ... .

[Last / Next] year in ... .
En ... del año [pasado / que viene].

Toward the beginning of ...
A principios de ... .

Toward the end of ... .
A finales de ... .

January	enero	July	julio
February	febrero	**August**	agosto
March	marzo	**September**	septiembre
April	abril	**October**	octubre
May	mayo	**November**	noviembre
June	junio	**December**	diciembre

Appendix B: A Few More Phrases

THINK POSITIVE

That's okay.
Está bien.

Cool!
¡Está bien!

Wonderful!
¡Fantástico!

(That's) super!
¡(Es) super!

(That's) great!
¡(Es) genial!

(That's) wild!
¡(Es) brutal!

Wow!
¡Wow!

What a riot!
¡Vaya juerga!

Thank god.
Gracias a dios.

That's interesting.
Qué interesante.

How exciting.
Qué emocionante.

[You're / She's] a nice girl.
[Eres / Es] una buena chica.

[You're / He's] a nice guy.
[Eres / Es] un buen chico.

That's very nice of you.
Muy amable de tu parte.

That's right.
Es cierto.

You're right.
Tienes razón.

BAD NEWS

That's too bad.
Qué lástima.

What a shame.
Qué pena.

What a bitch!
¡Qué putada! *(situation)*
¡Qué hija de puta! *(woman; see also Hot! WordList, p. 125).*

What a drag!
¡Qué lata! *(situation) or*
¡Qué [pesado / pesada]! *(person)*

That's the pits.
Qué desastre.

I don't give a [damn / shit].
Me importa un [bledo / pito].

Too bad for you.
Peor para ti.

That's wrong.
No es cierto.

You're wrong.
No tienes razón.

Damn!
¡Hostia!

Bullshit!
¡Una mierda!

Shit!
¡Mierda!

How tacky.
Qué mal gusto.

That's disgusting.
Qué asco.

What a sleaze.
Qué [vicioso / viciosa].

What a jerk. *(male or female)*
Qué gilipollas.

You're so stuck up.
Eres [un engreído / una engreída].

[He / She] is so stuck up.
Es [un engreído / una engreída].

[That / He / She] drives me crazy.
[Eso / Él / Ella] me vuelve [loco / loca].
(if you're a guy, say loco; *if a girl,* loca)*

Shut up!
¡Cállate!

SEE ALSO *INSULTS, PARTS I & II* (P. 85).

THIS & THAT

Your fly is open.
Tienes la bragueta abierta.

Really?
¿De verdad?

Exactly.
Exactamente.

Of course.
Claro.

I know.
Lo sé.

I don't know.
No lo sé.

I think so.
Creo que sí.

I don't think so.
Creo que no.

Oh, come on!
¡Venga ya!

You don't say!
¡No me digas!

You're kidding!
¡Anda ya!

Just kidding.
Era una broma.

I'm not kidding.
En serio.

That's (really) unbelievable.
Es (totalmente) increíble.

Give me a break.
No me tomes el pelo.

Very funny. *(ironic)*
Muy gracioso.

Oh my god.
Dios mío.

It doesn't matter.
No importa.

[Forget it / Fuck it].
Olvídalo.

SPECIAL OCCASIONS

Congratulations!
¡Felicidades!

Happy Birthday!
¡Feliz cumpleaños!

Happy Anniversary!
¡Feliz aniversario!

Merry Christmas!
¡Felices Navidades!

Happy New Year!
¡Feliz Año Nuevo!

Happy Valentine's Day!
¡Feliz día de los enamorados!

Good luck.
Buena suerte.

[Bon voyage / Have a good trip].
Buen viaje.

Gesundheit!
¡Jesús! *(Sp.)* or ¡Salud! *(L.A.)*

Appendix C: People & Places

NATIONALITIES, ETC.

REMEMBER: WORDS NOT MARKED WITH A FEMININE VARIANT (/-A) STAY THE SAME FOR BOTH GUYS AND GIRLS.

I am ... .
Soy ... .

Are you ... ?
¿Eres ... ?

Is [he/she] ... ?
¿Es ... ?

African africano (/-a)	**Asturian** asturiano (/-a)	**Bulgarian** búlgaro (/-a)	**Colombian** colombiano (/-a)
Algerian argelino (/-a)	**Australian** australiano (/-a)	**Canadian** canadiense	**Costa Rican** costarricense
American americano (/-a); norteamericano (/-a)	**Austrian** austriaco (/-a)	**from the Caribbean** caribeño (/-a)	**Croatian** croata
Andalusian andaluz (/-a)	**Basque** vasco (/-a)	**Castillian** castellano (/-a)	**Cuban** cubano (/-a)
Antillean antillano (/-a)	**Belgian (Walloon)** belga (valón [/-a])	**Catalan** catalán (/-a)	**Czech** checo (/-a)
Arab árabe	**Belgian (Flemish)** belga (flamenco [/-a])	**Central American** centroamericano (/-a)	**Danish** danés (/-a)
Argentine argentino (/-a)	**Bolivian** boliviano (/-a)	**Chilean** chileno (/-a)	**Dominican** dominicano (/-a)
Armenian armenio (/-a)	**Brazilian** brasileño (/-a)	**Chinese** chino (/-a)	**Dutch** holandés (/-a)
			Ecuadoran ecuatoriano (/-a)

Egyptian egipcio (/-a)	**Gypsy / Romany** [gitano (/-a) / romaní]	**Irish** irlandés (/-a)	**Macedonian** macedonio (/-a)
from El Salvador salvadoreño (/-a)	**Haitian** haitiano (/-a)	**Israeli** israelita	**Mexican** mexicano (/-a)
English inglés (/-a)	**Hispanic** hispano (/-a)	**Italian** italiano (/-a)	**Moroccan** marroquí
from Equatorial Guinea de la Guinea Ecuatorial	**Honduran** hondureño (/-a)	**Jamaican** jamaicano (/-a)	**mulatto** mulato (/-a)
Estonian estonio (/-a)	**from Hong Kong** de Hong Kong	**Japanese** japonés (/-a)	**from New Zealand** de Nueva Zelanda
Filipino filipino (/-a)	**Hungarian** húngaro (/-a)	**Jewish** judío (/-a)	**Nicaraguan** nicaragüense
Finnish finlandés (/-a)	**Icelandic** islandés (/-a)	**Korean** coreano (/-a)	**Nigerian** nigeriano (/-a)
French francés (/-a)	**Indian** *(from India)* de la India	**[Latin / Latino / Latina]** latino (/-a)	**Norwegian** noruego (/-a)
Galician gallego (/-a)	**[Indian / Native American]** indio (/-a)	**Latvian** letón (/-a)	**Panamanian** panameño (/-a)
German alemán (/-a)	**Indonesian** indonesio (/-a)	**Lebanese** libanés (/-a)	**Paraguayan** paraguayo (/-a)
Greek griego (/-a)	**Iranian** iraní	**Lithuanian** lituano (/-a)	**Peruvian** peruano (/-a)
Guatemalan guatemalteco (/-a)	**Iraqi** iraquí	**Luxemburguese** luxemburgués (/-a)	**Polish** polaco (/-a)
			Polynesian polinesio (/-a)

Portuguese portugués (/-a)	**Serbian** serbio (/-a)	**Swedish** sueco (/-a)	**Ukrainian** ucranio (/-a)
Puerto Rican puertorriqueño (/-a)	**from Singapore** de Singapur	**Swiss** suizo (/-a)	**Uruguayan** uruguayo (/-a)
[Québecois / French Canadian] [quebequés (/-a) / francocanadiense]	**Slovak** eslovaco (/-a)	**Taiwanese** taiwanés (/-a)	**Valencian** valenciano (/-a)
	Slovenian esloveno (/-a)	**Thai** tailandés (/-a)	**Venezuelan** venezolano (/-a)
Romanian rumano (/-a)	**South African** surafricano (/-a)	**Tunisian** tunecino (/-a)	**Vietnamese** vietnamita
Russian ruso (/-a)	**South American** sudamericano (/-a)	**Turkish** turco (/-a)	**Welsh** galés (/-a)
Scottish escocés (/-a)	**Spanish** español (/-a)	**from the U.S.** de los Estados Unidos	**from Zimbabwe** de Zimbabwe

A LITTLE GEOGRAPHY

NOTE: MOST PLACE NAMES WHICH ARE THE SAME IN BOTH LANGUAGES ARE NOT GIVEN.

Canada - Canadá
Central America - Centroamérica
Dominican Republic - la República Dominicana
England - Inglaterra
Great Britain - Gran Bretaña
Havana - La Habana

Ireland - Irlanda
London - Londres
New York - Nueva York
New Zealand - Nueva Zelanda
North America - [Norteamérica / América del Norte]
Northern Ireland - Irlanda del Norte
Scotland - Escocia
Seville - Sevilla
South Africa - Suráfrica
South America - Sudamérica
Spain - España
United States (of America) - Estados Unidos (de América)
Wales - Gales

Appendix D:
A Fast 'n' Dirty Guide to Spanish

Nobody likes grammar, but if you're really serious about speaking and being understood, you should check out this section at least once. Naturally, we don't expect you'll start babbling like a native right off the bat, but it can help to get a handle on how the language works.

First, some background: Spanish *(español)*, a Romance tongue evolved from Latin, is also known as Castilian *(castellano)* after Castile, the region in Spain where it developed. It's the official language there and in 17 countries in Latin America, though it's sometimes used alongside regional languages (like Basque, Catalan and Galician in Spain, Quechua in Peru, and Náhuatl and Maya in Mexico). Spanish is also one of the easiest languages for English speakers to learn, and its grammar is pretty regular. Here's a quick rundown:

NOUNS

Nouns, as you know, are words that name a person, place or thing. In Spanish, nouns have one of two genders—masculine and feminine—even for inanimate objects. So for example "sex" is masculine *(el sexo)*, and "blowjob" is feminine *(la mamada)*. Whether a word is masculine or feminine isn't always logical: *polla* ("cock") is feminine and *chocho* ("cunt") is masculine. There's an easy way to remember genders: Most masculine nouns end in "-o" or a consonant (once in a while they'll end in "-a," such as *el atleta*). Most feminine nouns simply end in "-a." Need a plural? Add "-s" (or sometimes "-es") at the end of the word *(la polla* becomes *las pollas* and *el chocho* becomes *los chochos)*.

ARTICLES

The definite article "the" has four forms in Spanish: for masculine words, *el* and its plural *los*; for feminine words, *la* and its plural *las*. The indefinite articles "a" or "an" have four parallel forms: *un* (masculine singular), *unos* (masculine plural), *una* (feminine singular), and *unas* (feminine plural).

PRONOUNS

yo	I
tú	you *(inf. sing.)*
usted	you *(formal sing.)*
él	he
ella	she
nosotros	we *(male or mixed)*
nosotras	we *(female only)*
vosotros	you *(inf. pl., male or mixed, in Sp.)*
vosotras	you *(inf. pl., female only, in Sp.)*
ustedes	you *(formal pl. in Sp.; gen. pl. in L.A.)*
ellos	they *(male or mixed)*
ellas	they *(female only)*

Here are the pronouns (words that replace nouns) in Spanish. Notice that "you" has four forms: singular, plural, formal and informal. Use *tú* or *vosotros* (informal) with friends, relatives and people your own age; for an older person or someone you respect, use *usted* or *ustedes*. Keep in mind that these days, at least in Spain, many people are dropping the formality and using *tú* in many cases. In Latin America, on the other hand, *usted* is better in more formal situations, and *vosotros* isn't used at all; for the plural, say *ustedes* to everyone, whether friends or strangers.

Sorry to break the news, but Spanish grammar is not "politically correct": *ellos* (they) is a group of guys and *ellas* is a group of girls, but if you have a mixed group, it's *ellos*. Same goes for [*nosotros / nosotras*] and [*vosotros / vosotras*].

DIRECT AND INDIRECT OBJECT PRONOUNS

These are the words that receive the action of the verb. For example, "him" in "I kiss him" is the direct object; "her" in "He gives her a kiss" is the indirect object and "a kiss" is the direct object. Like English, Spanish has different forms for these grammatical cases. Unlike in English, they mostly come *before* the verb, not after, so *Ella me besa* is literally "She me kisses" and *Él me lo da* is "He to me it gives." Don't worry, after a while it really will seem natural.

Note that some forms, like *le* or *los,* are used for different pronouns (*le* can mean "to him," "to her" or "to you"), so you have to look at the context to figure out who's doing what to whom.

	DIRECT OBJECT		INDIRECT OBJECT	
me	me	Me besa.	me	Me da un beso.
you (inf.)	te	Te besa	te	Te da un beso.
you (formal)	lo	Lo besa.	le	Le da un beso.
him	lo	Lo besa.	le	Le da un beso.
her	la	La besa.	le	Le da un beso.
us	nos	Nos besa.	nos	Nos da un beso.
you (inf. pl.)	os	Os besa.	os	Os da un beso.
you (formal pl.)	los	Los besa.	les	Les da un beso.
them (masc.)	los	Los besa.	les	Les da un beso.
them (fem.)	las	Las besa.	les	Les da un beso.

POSSESSIVE PRONOUNS

Just like in English, the pronouns have possessive forms. Most of them don't change for masculine or feminine nouns, but they do add an "-s" for the plural:

my	mi	our	[nuestro (masc.) / nuestra (fem.)]
your (inf.)	tu	your (inf. pl.)	[vuestro (masc.) / vuestra (fem.)]
your (formal)	su	your (formal pl.)	su (masc. & fem.)
[his / her]	su	their	su (masc. & fem.)

How do you know when it's *nuestro* or *nuestra*? It depends not on the gender of the person talking, but the gender of the word it's modifying. "Our house" is *nuestra casa* (feminine), but "our hotel" is *nuestro hotel* (masculine). And add an "-s" for the plural: *nuestras casas, nuestros hoteles*.

ADJECTIVES

Most often they come *after* the noun ("a pretty face" is *una cara bonita* instead of *una bonita cara*). The endings on Spanish adjectives also change for gender ("-o" goes to "-a" in the feminine) and plural (add "-s" or "-es"), though some change only for plurals. On the next page are a few examples:

	MASC.	MASC. PL.	FEM.	FEM. PL.
goodlooking	guapo	guapos	guapa	guapas
nice	simpático	simpáticos	simpática	simpáticas
affectionate	cariñoso	cariñosos	cariñosa	cariñosas
American	americano	americanos	americana	americanas
English	inglés	ingleses	inglesa	inglesas
easy	fácil	fáciles	fácil	fáciles
exciting	excitante	excitantes	excitante	excitantes

One neat thing: Spanish adjectives can act as nouns—just stick an article ("the" or "a") in front. For example *cariñosa* is "affectionate"; *una cariñosa* is "an affectionate girl." *Guapo* is "goodlooking"; *el guapo* is "the goodlooking guy."

VERBS

Verbs in Spanish are conjugated, which means they take different endings depending on who is doing the action and whether it's in the present, past, future, etc. Lucky for you, these endings are usually regular and easy to predict. There are three types of verbs, ending in "-ar," "-er" or "-ir." To conjugate them, drop the "-ar," "-er" or "-ir" and add the endings, like this:

THE PRESENT TENSE

	BESAR (to kiss)	COMER (to eat)	ABRIR (to open)
yo	bes- + **o**	com- + **o**	abr- + **o**
tú	bes- + **as**	com- + **es**	abr- + **es**
usted	bes- + **a**	com- + **e**	abr- + **e**
[él / ella]	bes- + **a**	com- + **e**	abr- + **e**
[nosotros / nosotras]	bes- + **amos**	com- + **emos**	abr- + **imos**
[vosotros / vosotras]	bes- + **áis**	com- + **éis**	abr- + **ís**
ustedes	bes- + **an**	com- + **en**	abr- + **en**
[ellos / ellas]	bes- + **an**	com- + **en**	abr- + **en**

In Spanish you don't have to use the pronoun like we do in English unless you want to make a point of who's doing the action or it's unclear from the context. For "I love you" you'll hear *Te quiero* more than *Yo te quiero*. But *Me quiere* can mean "He loves me" or "She loves me," so unless you're already sure who's doing the loving here, you might want to tack on *él* or *ella*.

THE PAST TENSE

	BESAR (to kiss)	COMER (to eat)	ABRIR (to open)
yo	bes- + **é**	com- + **í**	abr- + **í**
tú	bes- + **aste**	com- + **iste**	abr- + **iste**
usted	bes- + **ó**	com- + **ió**	abr- + **ió**
[él / ella]	bes- + **ó**	com- + **ió**	abr- + **ió**
[nosotros / nosotras]	bes- + **amos**	com- + **imos**	abr- + **imos**
[vosotros / vosotras]	bes- + **asteis**	com- + **isteis**	abr- + **isteis**
ustedes	bes- + **aron**	com- + **ieron**	abr- + **ieron**
[ellos / ellas]	bes- + **aron**	com- + **ieron**	abr- + **ieron**

THE FUTURE TENSE

yo voy	[nosotros / nosotras] vamos
tú vas	[vosotros / vosotras] vais
usted va	ustedes van
[él / ella] va	[ellos / ellas] van

The future tense in Spanish isn't heard as much as *ir a* ("to go go") plus the infinitive—like we say "I'm *going to* eat" instead of "I *will* eat." In Spanish that would be *Voy a comer*. Got it?

TO BE

Spanish has two verbs for "to be": *ser* and *estar*. Don't flip out: Just remember that *ser* is for permanent conditions—such as *ser un hombre* ("to be a man") or *ser alta* ("to be tall"). *Estar* is for temporary conditions: *estar casada* ("to be married"), *estar en Madrid* ("to be in Madrid").

	SER	ESTAR
yo	soy	estoy
tú	eres	estás
usted	es	está
[él / ella]	es	está
[nosotros / nosotras]	somos	estamos
[vosotros / vosotras]	sois	estáis
ustedes	son	están
[ellos / ellas]	son	están

PRESENT PARTICIPLE (GERUND)

Another handy tense is like the English "-ing." We usually say "I am kissing" to describe the kiss we're giving right now. In Spanish, use *estar* plus an "-ar" verb with the suffix *-ando,* or an "-er" or "-ir" verb with the suffix *-iendo.*

I'm kissing.	Estoy bes**ando**. (from *besar*)
You're opening.	Estás abr**iendo**. (from *abrir*)
She's eating.	Ella está com**iendo**. (from *comer*)

REFLEXIVE VERBS

Some verbs also have particles like *me, te, se, nos* or *os* tacked on or coming right before them. This means the verb is "reflexive" and the action affects the subject of the verb. So *Yo beso* means "I kiss," but *Yo me beso* means "I kiss myself." Sometimes the reflexive particle can change the meaning of a word a lot; *correr* means "to run," but *correrse* means "to come, have an orgasm."

VERBS & NOUNS TOGETHER

One thing to remember: When a verb acts on a noun that's a living person, you have to put an *a* between them. "To kiss" is *besar* and "John" is *Juan,* but you can't say *besar Juan*; the correct way is *besar a Juan.*

A LITTLE RESPECT

By now you've probably noticed that it's easy to show respect or distance to someone you don't know well by using the *usted* form—just take the "-s" off the *tú* form of the verb (which we give you throughout the book). So to hook up with a hot-shot ambassador, say *¿Tiene un cigarrillo?* instead of *¿Tienes un cigarrillo?* If the verb's reflexive, substitute *se* for *te: ¿Cómo se llama, señor?,* not *¿Cómo te llamas?* And with indirect object pronouns, substitute *le* for *te:* say *¿Le gusta?* instead of *¿Te gusta?*

FINALLY...

There are plenty of other verb tenses in Spanish, but the basic ones above will get you through most situations not covered in our phrases. Don't be afraid to make mistakes. The key to communication is to *try.* After all, you're a foreigner; if you can't conjugate like Cervantes—or even Julio Iglesias—people will understand. So relax, have a good time and *¡buen viaje!*

Appendix E: Hot! WordList

As in the rest of the book, words or phrases separated by a slash between brackets are an [either / or] choice; words or phrases in parentheses are an option—you can use them or drop them. Some examples: [el compañero / la compañera] gives you the masculine and feminine forms of "companion," a noun; however, *adulto* ("adult") is both noun and adjective, so you have the masculine and feminine forms in brackets, with (el) and (la) in parentheses (because you have the option of using the word as a noun): [(el) adulto / (la) adulta]. (Note that we always give you the article *el* or *la*, so you'll know immediately if a noun is masculine or feminine.) For adjectives that change the final "-o" to "-a," we indicate the feminine form with (/-a): *abusivo (/-a)*. Finally, in some cases personal names *(María, José)* are added in parentheses to show you how to use a word.

abdomen
n. el ábdomen
[abdominals / abs]
n. los (músculos) abdominales
abortion
n. el aborto
  to have an abortion
  hacerse un aborto
abstinent
adj. abstinente
abuse
n. el abuso
v. abusar
  emotional abuse
  el abuso emocional
  physical abuse
  el abuso físico
  sexual abuse
  el abuso sexual
abusive
adj. abusivo (/-a)
AC-DC
adj. bi, bisexual

  to be AC-DC
  darle a los dos palos, jugar en los dos campos, ser bisexual
acquaintance *(person)*
n. [el conocido / la conocida]
acquainted, to get (with Michael)
v. conocer (a Miguel)
Acquired Immune Deficiency Syndrome (AIDS)
n. el Síndrome de la Inmunodeficiencia Adquirida (SIDA)
adore
v. adorar
adult
n. & adj. [(el) adulto / (la) adulta]
  adult bookstore
  el sex-shop
adulterer
n. [el adúltero / la adúltera]
adulterous
adj. adúltero (/-a)
adultery
n. el adulterio

adventure *(sexual / gen.)*
n. la aventura
affair *(romance)*
n. la aventura, el lío,
el romance
   extramarital affair
   la relación extramatrimonial,
   la relación adulterina
   to have an affair (with)
   tener un lío, enredarse (con)
affection
n. el afecto, el cariño
affectionate
adj. afectuoso (/-a), cariñoso (/-a)
AIDS
n. el SIDA
aloof
adj. reservado (/-a)
amorous
adj. amoroso (/-a)
anal
adj. anal
   anal sex
   el sexo anal, la sodomía
androgynous
adj. andrógino (/-a)
anniversary
n. el aniversario
anus
n. el ano *(see also "asshole")*
aphrodisiac
n. & adj. (el) afrodisíaco (/-a)
areola
n. la aréola
arm
n. el brazo

armpit
n. el sobaco
arousal
n. la excitación
arouse
v. excitar
aroused
adj. excitado (/-a)
arousing
adj. excitante
asexual
adj. asexual
ass
n. el culo, el trasero
   hot ass
   el culo sexy
   piece of ass
   el cacho de carne
   to get some ass
   mojar
   to [lick / tongue] (her) ass
   lamer(le) el culo
   to shake one's ass
   menear el culo
asscheeks
n. las nalgas
assfuck
n. la follada por el culo, el sexo anal,
el coito anal *(med.)*
v. dar por el culo, follar por el culo,
encular, sodomizar
asshole
n. el ojo del culo, el ano *(body part)*;
[el / la] gilipollas *(jerk)*
   asshole buddy
   el amigote, el amiguete

athletic
adj. atlético (/-a)
attractive
adj. atractivo (/-a)
   to find (s.o.) attractive
   encontrar (a alg.) atractivo (/-a)
B&D
n. la esclavitud y la disciplina
babe
n. [nene / nena] *(Sp.)*, [papi / mami]
(L.A.) (in direct address); [el muñeco /
la muñeca] *(describing someone)*
baby *(term of endearment)*
n. [el niño / la niña]
bachelor
n. el soltero
   bachelor pad
   el piso de soltero
   bachelor party
   la despedida de soltero
   confirmed bachelor
   el solterón empedernido
back
n. la espalda
   on one's back
   boca arriba
backside
n. el trasero, el culo
bald
adj. calvo
bald spot
n. la calva
baldness
n. la calvicie
ball
v. see "fuck"

balls
n. los huevos *("eggs")*, los cojones,
las pelotas
   to have blue balls
   tenerlas hinchadas
ballsac
n. los huevos, el escroto *("scrotum")*
bar
n. el bar
   to bar hop
   ir de bares
   [the bar scene / the bars]
   los bares
   singles bar
   el bar de ligue
bareback *(without a condom)*
adv. a pelo
base, to get to first
v. alcanzar la primera etapa
beard
n. la barba
bearded
adj. con barba, barbudo
   bearded guy
   el barbas, el chico con barba
beat
v. pegar, golpear
beating
n. la paliza
beat off
v. hacerse una paja, meneársela,
machacársela
beau
n. el galán
beautiful
adj. bello (/-a), bonito (/-a)

beauty
n. la belleza, la preciosidad ("She's a beauty"—"Es una preciosidad")
beaver
n. el conejo ("rabbit"; see also "cunt")
bed
n. la cama
   bed partner
   [el compañero / la compañera] de cama
   to bedhop
   ir de cama en cama
   to go to bed (with John)
   acostarse (con Juan)
beefcake
n. el bonbón de calendario ("calendar candy")
belly
n. el vientre, la barriga; la panza (paunch)
belly button
n. el ombligo
beloved
n. & adj. [(el) querido / (la) querida], [(el) amado / (la) amada]
bestiality
n. la bestialidad
betrothal
n. los esponsales, los desposorios
betrothed
adj. & n. [(el) prometido / (la) prometida]
(my) better half
n. (mi) media naranja ("my half orange")
biceps
n. el bíceps

bigamist
n. [el bígamo / la bígama]
bigamous
adj. bígamo (/-a)
bigamy
n. la bigamia
biker
n. [el / la] biker
bikini
n. el bikini
   bikini briefs
   las bragas de bikini *(Sp.)*, los calzoncillos de bikini *(L.A.)*
   string bikini
   el tanga
bimbo
n. el bombón, la maciza tonta
   blonde bimbo
   la rubia platino
birth control
n. el control de la natalidad
adj. anticonceptivo (/-a)
   (birth control) pill
   la píldora (anticonceptiva)
   to be on the (birth control) pill
   tomar la píldora
[bisexual / bi]
adj. [bisexual / bi] *(see also "AC-DC")*
bisexuality
n. la bisexualidad
bitch
n. la bruja ("witch"), la víbora ("viper"), la hija de puta ("daughter-of-a-bitch")
v. joder, putear, quejarse, protestar ("He's always bitching"—"Siempre está jodiendo.")

bitchy *(woman)*
adj. ácida, quejosa, protestona, quisquillosa
bite
n. el mordisco
v. morder
  love bite
  el chupetón, el mordisco
blind date
n. la cita con alguien desconocido ("date with someone unknown")
[blond / blonde]
n. & adj. [(él) rubio / (la) rubia]
  dumb blonde
  la rubia platino
blow
v. see "suck"
blow job
n. la mamada
body
n. el cuerpo
  body odor
  el olor corporal
  body piercing
  el poner pendientes en el cuerpo ("to put rings on the body")
bombshell
n. el pedazo de mujer ("She's a bombshell"—"Es un pedazo de mujer")
bondage (and discipline)
n. la esclavitud (y la disciplina)
boner
n. see "hard-on"
boobs
n. see "tits"
bordello
n. el burdel, la casa de putas, el puticlub

bosom
n. el pecho, los pechos, los senos
  bosom buddy
  el amigo íntimo, el amiguete
bottom
n. el trasero *(see also "ass")*
boxer shorts
n. los calzoncillos
boy
n. el chico, el muchacho, el niño *(child)*
  boy toy
  el "juguete"
  party boy
  el parrandero, el juerguista
boyfriend
n. el novio, el amigo
boyish
adj. juvenil, jovencito, de niño
[bra / brassiere]
n. el sujetador, el sostén
break up
n. la separación
v. separarse
breast
n. el pecho, el seno
bridal
adj. nupcial
  bridal shower
  la despedida de soltera ("farewell to the single woman")
  bridal suite
  el suite nupcial
bride
n. la novia, la desposada
briefs
n. el slip, las bragas *(Sp.)*; los calzoncillos *(L.A.)*

buddy
n. el compañero, el amiguete

built
adj. macizo (/-a), cachas *(Sp.)*
("Charles is really built"—"Carlos está cachas")

bulge *(crotch)*
n. el paquete *("package")*
　　to show off one's bulge
　　marcar paquete

buns
n. las nalgas

burly
adj. fuerte, fornido

bush *(pubic)*
n. la pelambre, la pelambrera

bust
n. el busto, el pecho

bustier
n. el corpiño

busty
adj. pechugona

butt
n. see "ass" or "bottom"

buttfuck
n. & v. see "assfuck"

buttocks
n. las nalgas

buxom
adj. pechugona, rolliza, metida en carnes

care [for / about] (Lawrence)
v. querer (a Lorenzo)

caress
n. la caricia
v. acariciar

caring
adj. cariñoso (/-a)

carnal
adj. carnal

catch
n. el buen partido, la pesca ("Ann's a good catch"—"Ana es un buen partido")

celibate
adj. célibe, soltero (/-a)

celibacy
n. el celibato, la soltería

chap
n. see "guy"

charm
n. el encanto

to charm (Frank)
v. encantar (a Paco)

charming
adj. encantador (/-a)

chaste
adj. casto (/-a)

chastity
n. la castidad, el pudor
　　chastity belt
　　el cinturón de castidad

chauvinist, male
n. el machista

cheat (on Hank)
v. engañar, ponerle los cuernos (a Enrique)

cheek
n. la mejilla *(face)*; la nalga *(rear end)*

cheesecake
n. el bonbón de calendario *("calendar candy")*

cherry
n. la virginidad

to take (Rosie's) cherry
desflorar, tomarle la virginidad
(a Rosita)

chest
n. el pecho
  flat chest
  el pecho plano, el pecho liso
  hairy chest
  el pecho peludo

chick
n. la chica, la tía, la nena, la titi,
la moza

chlamydia
n. las clamídeas

chubby
adj. llenito (/-a), gordinflón (/-a),
rechoncho (/-a)

circumcised
adj. circuncidado (/-a)

clap
n. las purgaciones, la gonorrea
  to get the clap
  v. coger unas purgaciones

cleavage
n. el escote

climax
n. el clímax, el orgasmo
v. tener un orgasmo, correrse, irse

clitoral
adj. del clítoris, clitoriano (/-a)
  clitoral glans
  el glande clitoriano

[clitoris / clit]
n. el clítoris

club
n. el club

nightclub
el nightclub

sex club
el sex-club, el club erótico, el antro

cock
n. la polla, el pito, el rabo, el cuero,
el nabo, la verga, el miembro, el cipote,
el pico, la porra, el churro *(Mex.)*, el
bicho *(P.R. & Cuba)*, la pinga *(Cuba)*
  to be cock-crazy
  ser un chocholoco
  cockcheese
  el requesón
  cockhead
  el capullo, el glande
  cocksucker
  la chupapollas, la mamona
  cocktease
  la calientapollas
  horsecock
  el pollón

coitus
n. el coito
  coitus interruptus
  el coitus interruptus, el coito
  interrumpido

cold *(emotionally)*
adj. frío (/-a)

collar
n. el collar

[come / cum]
n. el semen, la leche
v. correrse, irse

come-on
n. el pase, el piropo
  come on to
  hacer un pase, piropear, trabajarse

commitment
n. la dedicación
   fear of commitment
   el miedo a comprometerse
companion
n. [el compañero / la compañera]
compliment
n. el cumplido *(gen.)*, el piropo *(spec. sexual)*
condom
n. el condón, el preservativo, la goma
   female condom
   el condón femenino
conquer (Annie) *(sexually or emotionally)*
v. conquistar (a Anita)
conquest
n. la conquista
consent
n. el consentimiento
   age of consent
   la mayoría de edad
considerate
adj. considerado (/-a)
contraception
n. la contracepción
contraceptive
n. & adj. (el) contraceptivo (/-a), (el) anticonceptivo (/-a)
   contraceptive cream
   la crema anticonceptiva
   contraceptive foam
   la espuma anticonceptiva
   contraceptive gel
   la jalea anticonceptiva
   the (contraceptive) pill
   la píldora (anticonceptiva)

   contraceptive sponge
   la esponja anticonceptiva
conjugal
adj. conyugal
copulate (with Bill)
v. copular (con Guillermo)
copulation
n. la copulación
coquette *(female)*
n. la coqueta
corrupt
v. corromper, pervertir
corrupted
adj. corrompido (/-a), pervertido (/-a)
corruptor
n. [el corruptor / la corruptora]
couple
n. la pareja
v. copular *(sexually)*
   married couple
   la pareja casada
court (Sophie)
v. cortejar, hacerle la corte (a Sofía)
courtship
n. el cortejo, el noviazgo
coy, to be *(woman)*
v. hacerse la interesante
[crabs / crab lice / pubic lice]
n. las ladillas
crack (of ass)
n. la raja (del culo)
cradle robber
n. [el / la] robacríos
crap
n. la caca, la mierda
v. cagar

cross dress
v. travestirse
cross-dresser
n. [el travestido / la travestida],
el travesti
crotch
n. la entrepierna, los bajos
cruise (Beth)
v. ligar (con Isabel), trabajarse
(a Isabel)
cruising
n. el ligoteo, el ligue
  to·go cruising
  ir de ligue, hacer la carrera
crush
n. el flechazo
  to have a crush (on)
  estar colgado (/-a), estar encaprichado (/-a) (por)
cuckold *(male)*
n. el cornudo
cuddle (with her)
v. acurrucarse, enroscarse (con ella)
cuddling
n. el acurrucarse, el enroscarse
cunnilingus
n. el cunnilingus
cunt
n. el chocho, el coño, el conejo,
la almeja, la concha *(Arg.)*, la chucha
(Chile), el bollo *(Cuba)*, la seta *(Mex.)*
  cunt juice
  el jugo del chocho, el flujo
  cunt lapper
  el lamechochos
  cunt lips
  los labios (del chocho)

  dry cunt
  el chocho seco
  wet cunt
  el chocho mojado
curvaceous
adj. exuberante, voluptuosa
cut *(penis)*
adj. circuncidado (/-a)
cute
adj. mono (/-a)
dance
n. el baile
v. bailar
[dark / dark-haired]
adj. moreno (/-a)
(my) darling
n. & adj. (mi) [querido / querida]
date
n. la cita (para salir)
v. salir con
  blind date
  el salir con alguien desconocido
  ("going out with someone unknown";
  no exact equiv.)
  date rape
  see "rape"
  to have a date (with Joan)
  tener cita, salir (con Juana)
double date
n. el salir los cuatro *("four going out";*
no exact equiv.)
v. salir los cuatro
debauched
adj. crápula, crapuloso (/-a)
debauchery
n. la crápula, el libertinaje,
la corrupción

deep kiss
n. & v. see "French kiss"

deep throat
v. tragarla [a fondo / toda / entera]

deflower
v. desflorar, desvirgar

degenerate
adj. degenerado (/-a)

den of iniquity
n. el antro de perdición

deviant
n. & adj. [(el) invertido / (la) invertida]
   sexual deviant
   [el invertido / la invertida] sexual

diaphragm
n. el diafragma

dick
n. see "cock"
v. see "fuck"

dildo
n. el consolador

dirty
adj. sucio (/-a), guarro (/-a),
pervertido (/-a)
   dirty joke
   el chiste verde ("green joke")
   dirty mind
   la mente pervertida
   dirty minded
   pervertido (/-a)
   dirty old man
   el viejo verde ("green old man")

disco(theque)
n. la discoteca

discreet
adj. discreto (/-a)

discretion
n. la discreción

divorce
n. el divorcio
v. divorciarse
   to divorce my [husband / wife]
   divorciarme de mi [esposo / mujer]

divorced
adj. divorciado (/-a)
   divorced man
   el divorciado
   [divorced woman / divorcée]
   la divorciada

do (Mary Carmen)
v. hacerlo (con Maricarmen)

doggy style *(sexual position)*
n. a cuatro patas

dominate
v. dominar

dominating
adj. dominador (/-a), dominante

dominator *(male)*
n. el dominador

dominatrix
n. la dominatriz, la dominadora

Don Juan
n. el Don Juan

double entendre
n. el doble sentido

douche
n. el douche, el lavado vaginal
v. lavarse (la vagina)

dreamboat *(male)*
n. el sueño, el sueño de tío ("He's a
dreamboat"—"Es un sueño de tío")

drunk
adj. borracho (/-a), mamado (/-a),
bebido (/-a)

to get drunk
emborracharse

dude
n. see "guy"

dungeon
n. la mazmorra, el calabozo, el antro

Dutch, go
v. pagar a la americana *("to pay American-style")*

ear
n. la oreja

earring
n. el pendiente

easy *(sexually)*
adj. fácil, facilón (/-a)

eat out
v. comer, lamer

ejaculate
v. eyacular

ejaculation
n. la eyaculación
   premature ejaculation
   la eyaculación precoz

elope
v. fugarse (para casarse)

embrace
n. el abrazo
v. abrazar
   to embrace each other
   abrazarse

emotion
n. la emoción

emotional
adj. emotivo (/-a)

enema
n. el enema, la lavativa

engaged
adj. prometido (/-a)
   to get engaged
   prometerse

engagement
n. el compromiso matrimonial
   engagement ring
   el anillo de compromiso

erect *(penis or nipples)*
adj. erecto (/-a), en erección, tieso (/-a)

erection
n. la erección, la polla tiesa

erogenous
adj. erógeno (/-a)
   erogenous zone
   la zona erógena

erotic
adj. erótico (/-a)

erotica
n. el material erótico

eroticism
n. el erotismo

escort
n. [el chico / la chica] de compañía
   escort service
   la agencia de [chicos / chicas] de compañía

ex
n. [el / la] ex
   ex-lover
   [el / la] ex-amante
   ex-husband
   el ex-marido
   ex-wife
   la ex-esposa
   ex-boyfriend
   el ex-novio

ex-girlfriend
la ex-novia
exhibitionism
n. el exhibicionismo
exhibitionist
n. [el / la] exhibicionista
exhibitionistic
adj. exhibicionista
experienced *(sexually)*
adj. experimentado (/-a)
extramarital affair
n. la relación extramatrimonial,
la relación adulterina, el lío
eye
n. el ojo
  to devour (Rachel) with one's eyes
  comerse (a Raquel) con los ojos
  to make eyes (at Chris)
  castigar con los ojos (a Cristóbal)
face
n. la cara
fair
adj. rubio (/-a) *(hair)*, blanco (/-a) *(skin)*
fair-haired
adj. rubio (/-a)
faithful
adj. fiel
falsies
n. los rellenos
fantasize
v. soñar, imaginar
fantasy
n. la fantasía erótica, el sueño erótico
fat
adj. gordo (/-a)
feel up
v. meter mano, toquetear

feelings
n. los sentimientos
fellate
v. hacer una felación *(see also "suck")*
fellatio
n. la felación
female
n. & adj. (la) hembra
feminine
adj. femenina
femininity
n. femineidad
femme fatale
n. la mujer fatal
fetish
n. el morbo, el fetiche
  foot fetish
  el morbo por los pies
  leather fetish
  el morbo por el cuero
fetishist
n. [el morboso / la morbosa],
[el / la] fetichista
  foot fetishist
  [el morboso / la morbosa] por los
  pies
  leather fetishist
  [el morboso / la morbosa] por el
  cuero
[fiancé *(male)* **/ fiancée** *(female)***]**
n. [el novio / la novia]
figure *(female)*
n. la figura
  full figure
  la figura llenita
  full-figured
  llenita

great figure
la figura estupenda
hourglass figure
la cintura de avispa *("wasp waist")*
finger
n. el dedo
v. tocar con los dedos, follar con los dedos *("finger-fuck")*
fit *(healthy)*
adj. en forma
flabby
adj. fofo (/-a)
flash
v. exhibirse
flasher *(male)*
n. el exhibicionista
flat-chested
adj. de pecho [plano / liso]
flatter (Terri)
v. halagar, darle coba (a Teresita)
flattered
adj. halagado (/-a)
flatterer
n. [el adulador / la aduladora]
flattery
n. los halagos, la adulación
flesh
n. la carne
fleshpot
n. la calentorra
fling
n. la aventura
to have a fling (with George)
tener una aventura (con Jorge)
flirt
n. [el coqueto / la coqueta]
v. flirtear, ligar

[flirtation / flirting]
n. el flirteo, el ligue
flirtatious
adj. coqueto (/-a)
fly *(of pants)*
n. la bragueta
fool around (with)
v. hacer un bollo, darse un revolcón, comerse una rosca (con)
to fool around (behind Steve's back)
ponerle los cuernos (a Esteban)
foreplay
n. los juegos preliminares
foreskin
n. el prepucio
to pull back the foreskin
descapullar
fornicate
v. fornicar
fornication
n. la fornicación
fox *(male & female)*
n. [el matador / la matadora]
foxy
adj. matador (/-a)
French kiss
n. el beso a la francesa, el beso húmedo, el beso atornillado, el morreo *(Sp.)*
v. besar a la francesa, darse un beso húmedo, darse un beso atornillado, morrear *(Sp.)*
friend
n. [el amigo / la amiga]
friendly
adj. amistoso (/-a)

friendship
n. la amistad
frigid
adj. frígida
frigidity
n. la frigidez
frottage
n. el magreo
fuck
n. el polvo, la follada, el revolcón
    to fuck (Jo)
    follar, joder, tirarse, echar un palo
    (a Pepa), echar un polvo (con Pepa),
    chingar (a Pepa) *(Mex.)*, coger
    (a Pepa) *(Arg.)*, singar (a Pepa) *(Cuba)*
fucked-out
adj. hecho (/-a) polvo
fucker *(male)*
n. el follador
fun
n. la diversión
adj. divertido (/-a)
G-spot
n. el punto ge
G-string
n. el tanga
gag (Phil)
v. amordazar (a Felipe)
gag (on your cock)
v. ahogarse, atragantarse (con tu polla)
gang bang (a woman)
n. la follada colectiva (a una mujer)
v. follar en grupo (a una mujer)
gang rape (a woman)
n. la violación colectiva (a una mujer)
v. violar en grupo (a una mujer)

[garter / garter belt]
n. el liguero
gay
n. & adj. [(el) / (la)] gay, [(el) / (la)]
homosexual *(see also "lesbian")*
genitals
n. los genitales, los órganos sexuales
gentleman
n. el caballero
gentlemanly
adj. caballeroso
get it on
v. see "fuck"
get it up
v. ponerse dura, ponerse tiesa, tener
una erección, hacerla levantarse
get laid
v. see "fuck"
gigolo
n. el gigolo, el chulo
girl
n. la chica, la tía, la muchacha,
la chavala, la niña *(child)*
    party girl
    la parrandera, la juerguista
girlfriend
n. la novia, la amiga
girlish
adj. aniñada, de niña
glans *(of penis)*
n. el capullo, el glande *(med.)*
go down on (Raoul)
v. chupar (a Raúl)
go steady (with Beatrice)
v. ir en serio (con Beatriz)
golddigger
n. [el interesado / la interesada],
[el aprovechado / la aprovechada]

golden showers
n. la "lluvia dorada"

gonorrhea
n. la gonorrea, las purgaciones *("clap")*

goodlooking
adj. guapo (/-a), bonito (/-a), bien parecido (/-a)

gorgeous
adj. fabuloso (/-a); superguapo (/-a); despampanante; de película *("out of a movie")*

groin
n. el empeine, la ingle *(see also "crotch")*

groom
n. el novio, el desposado

grope
n. el toqueteo, el manoseo
v. toquetear, manosear

group sex
n. la orgía

guy
n. el chico, el tipo, el tío, el muchacho

hair
n. el pelo, el cabello
  pubic hair
  el vello púbico, el pendejo *(L.A.) (a single hair)*; la pelambre, la pelambrera, los pendejos *(L.A.) ("bush")*

hairless
adj. de piel lisa, lampiño *(beardless)*

hairy
adj. peludo (/-a), velludo (/-a)

hand
n. la mano

handjob
n. la paja

to give [oneself / Pat] a handjob
[hacerse una paja / hacerle una paja a Patricio]

handcuff
v. poner las esposas

handcuffs
n. las esposas

handsome *(man)*
adj. guapo, bien parecido, hermoso

hangover
n. la resaca
  to have a hangover
  tener una resaca, estar de resaca

harass (sexually)
v. acosar (sexualmente)

sexual harassment
n. el acoso sexual

hard
adj. duro (/-a), tieso (/-a) *(penis)*
adv. a lo fuerte, a lo duro
  to get hard
  ponerse tiesa, ponerse dura, tener una erección, estar empalmado, estar armado
  hard body
  el cuerpo macizo

hard-to-get, to play
v. hacerse [el / la] interesante

hardcore
adj. duro (/-a) *(videos, books)*; de línea dura *(person)*
  hardcore guy
  el tipo de línea dura
  hardcore sex
  el sexo a lo duro

hard-on
n. la erección, la polla tiesa

to have a hard-on
tener la polla tiesa, tener una
erección, estar empalmado
[morning / piss] hard-on
la erección matinal
harem
n. el harén
harness
n. el arnés
hate
n. el odio
v. odiar
have (Louise) *(sexually)*
v. tirarse (a Luisa) *(see also "fuck")*
  have sex
  see "fuck"
head
n. la cabeza *(body part)*; el capullo
(penis); la mamada, la chupada *(blowjob)*
  to give (good) head
  chuparla (bien), mamarla (bien)
healthy
adj. sano (/-a)
heart
n. el corazón
  to break (Leonard's) heart
  partirle el corazón, romperle
  el corazón (a Leonardo)
  heartache
  el dolor, la pena
  heartbreak
  el corazón roto
  heartbreaker
  [el / la] rompecorazones
  heartbroken
  con el corazón roto

heartthrob *(male)*
el ídolo, el sex-symbol
heat
n. el calor
  to be in heat
  estar en celo
he-man
n. el macho
hemorrhoids
n. las hemorroides
hepatitis
n. la hepatitis
herpes
n. el herpes
heterosexual
n. & adj. [(el) / (la)] heterosexual
heterosexuality
n. la heterosexualidad
hickey
n. el chupetón, el mordisco
high *(on drugs)*
adj. drogado (/-a), colocado (/-a),
flipado (/-a)
  to get high
  drogarse, colocarse, fliparse
hips
n. las caderas, las cachas *(Sp.)*
hit
v. golpear, pegar
  to hit (on Dorothy)
  trabajarse, hacerle un pase
  (a Dorotea)
HIV (virus)
n. el VIH *(pron. "veh-ee-AH-cheh")*,
el virus del SIDA
  HIV-negative
  seronegativo (/-a), VIH-negativo (/-a)

HIV-positive
seropositivo (/-a), VIH-positivo (/-a)
HIV-status
no exact equiv. ("What's your HIV status?"—"¿Eres seropositivo (/-a)?")
hole *(body orifice)*
n. el agujero
   asshole *(body part)*
   el ojo del culo
homely
adj. feúcho (/-a)
homewrecker *(female)*
n. la robamaridos, la rompehogares, la ladrona de hombres, la "otra"
homosexual
n. & adj. [[el) / (la)] homosexual
homosexuality
n. la homosexualidad
honeymoon
n. la luna de miel *(post-wedding period)*; el viaje de novios *(post-wedding trip)*
hooker
n. la puta, la prostituta
horny
adj. caliente, cachondo (/-a) *(Sp.)*
hot
adj. sexy, erótico (/-a)
   to have the hots (for Andrew)
   estar caliente (por Andrés)
hot-to-trot
adj. caliente, cachondo (/-a)
   hot-to-trot girl
   la calentorra, la salida, la cachonda
   hot-to-trot guy
   el calentón, el salido, el cachondo

hug
n. el abrazo
v. abrazar
hump
v. see "fuck"
[hung / well-hung]
adj. bien dotado
hunk
n. el guapetón, el guapote, el tío guapo, el tipo bueno, el macizo
hunky
adj. bueno, macizo
hurt
v. herir, hacer daño
husband
n. el marido, el esposo
hussy
n. la fresca, la frescachona
hymen
n. el himen
immoral
adj. inmoral
immorality
n. la inmoralidad
impale
v. empalar, clavar *(see also "fuck")*
impolite
adj. maleducado (/-a)
impotence
n. la impotencia
impotent
adj. impotente
inconsiderate
adj. desconsiderado (/-a)
inexperienced *(sexually)*
adj. inexperto (/-a)

infatuated (with)
adj. encaprichado (/-a) (por)
infatuation (with)
n. el encaprichamiento (por)
infidelity
n. la infidelidad
ingenue
n. la ingenua
inhibited
adj. inhibido (/-a)
insatiable
adj. insaciable
intercourse *(sexual)*
n. las relaciones sexuales, el coito
intimacy
n. la intimidad
   fear of intimacy
   el miedo a la intimidad
intimate
adj. íntimo (/-a)
invite
v. invitar
   to invite Nuria (for coffee)
   invitar a Nuria (a tomar un café)
   to invite Nuria (to my house)
   invitar a Nuria (a mi casa)
invitation
n. la invitación
IUD (Intra-Uterine Device)
n. el DIU (dispositivo intra-uterino)
jack off
v. see "beat off"
jailbait
n. [el / la] menor (de edad)
jealous
adj. celoso (/-a)

jealousy
n. el celo, los celos
jerk *(person)*
n. [el / la] gilipollas
jerk off
v. see "beat off"
jilt
v. dejar plantado (/-a)
jism
n. see "[come / cum]"
jock
n. [el / la] atleta *(person)*; el soporte atlético *(jockstrap)*
   jockstrap
   el soporte atlético
john
n. el wáter, el lavabo *(toilet)*; el cliente (de una puta) *(whore's client)*
jugs
n. see "tits"
jump (Cathy's bones)
v. saltarle encima, atacar (a Catalina)
keep (a [man / mistress])
v. mantener (a [un querido / una querida])
kept
adj. mantenido (/-a)
   kept [man / woman]
   [el mantenido / la mantenida]
kink
n. el morbo, la guarrada
kinky
adj. morboso (/-a), vicioso (/-a), retorcido (/-a), rijoso (/-a)
kiss
n. el beso
v. besar

French kiss
n. el beso francés, el beso atornillado, el morreo *(Sp.)*
v. besar a la francesa, besar atornillado, morrear *(Sp.)*

knock up
v. dejar preñada, preñar

knocked up
adj. preñada

knockers
n. see "tits"

knot, to tie the (with Arthur)
v. ponerse los anillos (con Arturo)

labiae
n. los labios (de la vagina)

lady
n. la dama

   ladykiller
   el matador, el rompecorazones ("heartbreaker")

   lady's man
   el mujeriego, el faldero *(neg. connotation)*

   lady of the evening
   la mujer de la noche, la mujer de la vida, la mujer de la calle

   young lady
   señorita

ladylike
adj. femenina, como una señora

lascivious
adj. lascivo (/-a)

latex
n. el látex, la goma
adj. de látex

lay
n. el polvo, la follada, el revolcón
v. see "fuck"

[He's / She's] a great lay.
Folla bien.

lead (Rick) on
v. darle largas (a Ricardo)

lean *(not fat)*
adj. delgado (/-a)

leash
n. la correa (para perros)

leather
n. el cuero

   leather fetish
   el morbo por el cuero

[lecher / lech]
n. el obseso, el vicioso, el lascivo, el sátiro

lecherous
adj. lascivo (/-a)

leer
n. la mirada lasciva
v. mirar lascivamente, comerse con los ojos

leg
n. la pierna

leggy *(woman)*
adj. pernuda, pernilarga

lesbian
n. & adj. (la) lesbiana; (la) tortillera, (la) bollera ("dyke")

lewd
adj. lascivo (/-a), rijoso (/-a)

lewdness
n. lascividad, rijosidad

libidinous
adj. libidinoso (/-a)

libido
n. la libido

lice (pubic)
n. las ladillas
lick
n. el lametón
v. lamer
like
v. gustar
 I like you. *(physically)*
 Me gustas.
 I like you. *(personality)*
 Me caes muy bien.
lip
n. el labio
 cunt lips
 los labios de la vagina
Lolita
n. la nínfula
lonely
adj. solitario (/-a)
loose *(sexually)*
adj. golfo (/-a)
 loose [guy / girl]
 [el golfo / la golfa]
love
n. el amor
v. querer, amar *(more passionate)*
 my love
 mi amor
 to be in love (with)
 estar enamorado (/-a) (de)
 to fall in love (with Peter)
 enamorarse (de Pedro)
 to fall head over heels in love (with)
 enamorarse locamente, enamorarse patas arriba (de)
 love affair (with)
 la aventura, el lío, el romance (con)

love at first sight
el amor a primera vista
love birds
los tórtolos *("turtledoves")*
love bite
el chupetón, el mordisco
love 'em and leave 'em
picar y volar ("That guy loves 'em and leaves 'em"—"Ese pica y vuela")
love handles
los michelines
love letter
la carta de amor
love life
la vida amorosa, la vida sentimental
love nest
el nido de amor
love poem
el poema de amor
love potion
el filtro de amor, el afrodisiaco
love song
la canción de amor
 to make love ([to / with])
 hacer el amor (con)
 puppy love
 el amor de jovencitos, el amor de críos
loveable
adj. adorable
loveless
adj. sin amor
lovely
adj. encantador (/-a)
lover
n. [el / la] amante, [el enamorado / la enamorada]

lovers' lane
el picadero
lovers' quarrel
la pelea de amor, la riña de amor
lovesick (for Tom)
adj. enferma de amor (por Tomás),
tener el mal de amores (por Tomás)
loving
adj. cariñoso (/-a), amoroso (/-a)
[lubricant / lube]
n. el lubricante, la crema
lust
n. la lujuria, la lascivia
  to lust ([for / after] Susan)
  desear (a Susana), beber los vientos
  (por Susana), morir por los huesos
  (de Susana)
  lust-crazed
  loco (/-a) de deseo
lustful
adj. lujurioso (/-a), lascivo (/-a)
machismo
n. el machismo
macho
n. & adj. (el) macho, (el) viril,
(el) hombre
machista
n. & adj. (el) machista
madam
n. la señora *(polite)*; la madam
(prostitute)
make a move (on Ray)
v. hacer un pase (a Ramón)
make, to be on the
v. ir de ligue
make out (with Hope)
v. pegarse el lote, comerse una rosca
(con Esperanza)

make up
v. volver, arreglarse, reconciliarse
("Let's make up"—"Vamos a
arreglarnos")
  kiss and make up
  arreglarlo todo con un beso
male
n. & adj. (el) varón, (el) hombre,
(el) macho, masculino
  male chauvinist
  el machista
man
n. el hombre
  dirty old man
  el viejo verde *("green old man")*
  man-about-town
  el hombre de mundo, el hombre "in"
  older man
  el hombre mayor, el hombre maduro
manhood
n. la virilidad *(virility)*; la edad viril
(adulthood)
manly
adj. masculino, viril
marital
adj. marital
marriage
n. el matrimonio *(institution or married
couple)*; la boda *(wedding)*
  civil [marriage / wedding]
  [el matrimonio / la boda] civil
  common-law marriage
  el matrimonio consuetudinario
  loveless marriage
  el matrimonio sin amor
  marriage counselor
  [el consejero / la consejera]
  matrimonial

marriage of convenience
el matrimonio de conveniencia,
el matrimonio de interés
open marriage
el matrimonio abierto
unconsummated marriage
el matrimonio rato
married
adj. casado (/-a)
married couple
el matrimonio, la pareja casada,
los cónyuges
married life
la vida conyugal
[marry (Adam) / to get married (to Adam)]
v. casarse (con Adán)
masculine
adj. masculino, viril
masculinity
n. la masculinidad, la virilidad
masochism
n. el masoquismo
masochist
n. [el / la] masoquista, [el / la] masoca
masochistic
adj. masoquista, masoca
massage
n. el masaje
v. masajear, dar un masaje
master
n. el amo, el señor
masturbate
v. masturbar(se) *(see also "beat off")*
masturbation
n. la masturbación
mutual masturbation
la masturbación mutua

matchmaker
n. [el celestino / la celestina]
mate
n. la pareja, [el compañero /
la compañera], [el / la] cónyuge
v. aparear, acoplar(se)
mating rituals
n. los juegos de apareamiento,
el cortejo, el ritual del cortejo
matrimonial
adj. matrimonial, de boda
matrimony
n. see "marriage" or "wedding"
meat
n. la carne *(flesh)* ; la polla *(penis)*
(see also "cock")
to beat one's meat
n. see "beat off"
meat market
el bar de ligue, el picadero
member *(penis)*
n. el miembro *(see also "cock" and
"penis")*
ménage à trois
n. el trío, el ménage à trois
to have a ménage à trois
montar un trío
menopause
n. la menopausia
male menopause
la menopausia masculina,
la "pitopausia" *(hum.)*
menstruate
v. menstruar
menstruation
n. la menstruación

mind games (with Laura), to play
v. comerle el coco (a Laura)
minor (jailbait)
n. [el / la] menor (de edad)
missionary position
n. la postura de Adán *("Adam's position")*
mistress
n. la querida *(lover)*; la dominatriz *(dominatrix)*
modest
adj. modesto (/-a)
modesty
n. la modestia, el pudor
molest *(sexually)*
v. abusar (sexualmente), toquetear
molestation (sexual)
n. el abuso (sexual)
molester
n. el abusador (sexual)
monogamous
adj. monógamo (/-a)
monogamy
n. la monogamia
mons veneris *(female pubes)*
n. el monte de Venus
moral
adj. moral
morals
n. las morales
   loose morals
   la moral laxa, la manga ancha *("wide sleeve")*
mound of Venus
n. el monte de Venus
mount
v. montar *(see also "fuck")*

mouth
n. la boca
move (on Martha), to make a
v. [hacerle / echarle] un pase (a Marta)
muff
n. see "cunt"
   muff diver
   el comechochos
muscle
n. el músculo
muscular
adj. musculoso (/-a), cachas *(Sp.)*
mustache
n. el bigote
   guy with a mustache
   el bigotes, el bigotudo
nail *(sexually)*
v. clavar *(see also "fuck")*
naked
adj. desnudo (/-a), en pelotas, en cueros
   stark naked
   en cueros vivos
navel
n. el ombligo
neck
n. el cuello
v. besuquearse, acariciarse
necrophilia
n. la necrofilia
necrophiliac
n. [el necrófilo / la necrófila]
adj. necrofílico (/-a)
needy
adj. necesitado (/-a)
negligé
n. el negligé, el susana

nice
adj. simpático (/-a), majo (/-a) *(Sp.)*
nightclub
n. la discoteca, el nightclub
nightlife
n. la vida nocturna
nipple
n. el pezón
  nipple clip
  la pinza para los pezones
  nipple play
  el juguetear con los pezones
  nipple ring
  el pendiente de pezón, el anillo de pezón
  nipple torture
  la tortura de pezones
nocturnal emission
n. la polución nocturna *("nocturnal pollution")*
nude
n. & adj. [(el) desnudo / (la) desnuda]
  nude beach
  la playa nudista
nudism
n. el nudismo
nudist
n. & adj. [(el) / (la)] nudista, [(el) / (la)] naturalista
nudity
n. la desnudez
nuts
n. see "balls"
nylons
n. las medias, los panties
nymphet
n. la nínfula

nymphomania
n. la ninfomanía, el furor uterino *("uterine frenzy")*
[nymphomaniac / nympho]
n. la ninfómana
obey
v. obedecer
obscene
adj. obsceno (/-a)
  obscene phone call
  la llamada obscena
obscenity
n. la obscenidad
ogle (Sandra)
v. comerse (a Sandra) con los ojos
old
adj. viejo (/-a)
  old flame
  el antiguo amor *("old love")*
  old maid
  la solterona
one-night stand
n. el ligue de un día, el rollo de un día
open
v. abrir
adj. abierto (/-a), liberado (/-a)
  open marriage
  el matrimonio abierto
  open relationship
  la relación abierta, la pareja abierta
oral
adj. oral
  oral sex
  el sexo oral
orgasm
n. el orgasmo

to bring (Claire) to orgasm
hacer (a Clara) correrse
to have an orgasm
tener un orgasmo
multiple orgasm
el orgasmo múltiple
orgasmic
adj. orgásmico (/-a)
multiorgasmic
multiorgásmico (/-a)
orgy
n. la orgía
to have an orgy
montar una orgía
other
n. & adj. [(el) otro / (la) otra]
(my) other half
(mi) media naranja *("my half orange")*
the other [woman / man]
[la otra mujer / el otro hombre]
oversexed
adj. desatado (/-a), disparado (/-a)
pain
n. el dolor
painful
adj. doloroso (/-a)
panties *(women's)*
n. las bragas
partner *(romantic or sexual)*
n. [el compañero / la compañera]
bed partner
[el compañero / la compañera] de cama
domestic partner
[el compañero / la compañera]
party
n. la fiesta, el parrandeo, la pachanga

v. ir(se) de juerga, ir(se) de parranda, [estar / andar] de parranda, parrandear
dinner party
la cena
party animal
[el parrandero / la parrandera], [el / la] juerguista, [el pachanguero / la pachanguera]
pool party
la fiesta en la piscina
sex party
la orgía
singles party
la fiesta de solteros
pass *(sexual advance)*
n. el pase
to make a pass (at Agnes)
[hacerle / echarle] un pase (a Inés)
passion
n. la pasión
in the throes of passion
en la cima de la pasión
passionate
adj. apasionado (/-a)
paw
v. manosear, toquetear, magrear
pecker
n. see "cock"
[pectorals / pecs]
n. los pectorales
pedophile
n. el pedófilo
pedophilia
n. la pedofilia
pee
v. mear, hacer pis

peep show
n. el espectáculo porno en vivo
penetrate
v. penetrar
penile
adj. del pene
penis
n. el pene *(see also "cock")*
perineum
n. el perineo
period *(menstrual)*
n. la regla
　to have one's period
　tener la regla
[personal ads / the personals]
n. los anuncios personales,
los contactos
personality
n. la personalidad
pervert
n. [el pervertido / la pervertida]
v. pervertir
perverted
adj. pervertido (/-a), morboso (/-a) *(Sp.)*
pet
v. acariciarse
peter
n. see "cock"
phallic
adj. fálico (/-a)
　phallic symbol
　el símbolo fálico
phallus
n. el falo
phone sex
n. el sexo telefónico

physique
n. el físico
　muscular physique
　el físico musculoso
　shapely physique
　el físico bien formado
　slim physique
　el físico delgado
pick up (Chuck)
v. ligar (con Carlitos)
pierce
v. perforar, agujerear *(body or ear)*;
penetrar *(sexually)*
pierced
adj. agujereado (/-a)
　pierced ears
　las orejas agujereadas
　pierced nipple
　el pezón agujereado
piercing
n. la perforación
　body piercing
　el poner anillos en el cuerpo
　("to put rings on the body")
pill *(birth control)*
n. la píldora (anticonceptiva)
　to be on the pill
　tomar la píldora
pimp
n. el chulo, el alcahuete
v. alcahuetear
pin-up girl
n. el bonbón de calendario *("calendar candy")*
pinch
v. pellizcar
piss
n. el pis, la orina, la meada
v. mear, hacer pis

platonic
adj. platónico (/-a)
  platonic relationship
  la relación platónica
play (with)
v. jugar (con)
  to make a play for
  see "pass"
  to play doctor (with)
  jugar a los médicos, jugar a las
  casitas (con)
playboy
n. el "playboy"
playful
adj. juguetón (/-a)
pleasure
n. el gusto, el placer
  to give pleasure (to Evie)
  darle placer (a Evita)
pleasurable
adj. grato (/-a), agradable
pocket pool
n. la paja de bolsillo, el billar de bolsillo
(L.A.)
  to play pocket pool
  masturbarse a través del bolsillo,
  jugar al billar de bolsillo *(L.A.)*
polite
adj. educado (/-a), cortés *(masc. &
fem.)*
[porn / porno]
n. & adj. (el) porno
  porn mag(azine)
  la revista porno
  porn shop
  la tienda porno, el sex-shop

porn star
la estrella porno *(male or female)*
porn theater
el cine porno *(movies)*; el teatro
porno *(live acts)*
porn video
el vídeo porno
pornographic
adj. pornográfico (/-a)
pornography
n. la pornografía
postcoital
adj. de después del coito
  postcoital nausea
  la náusea de después del coito
[precome / precum]
n. el flujo, el goteo
pregnancy
n. el embarazo
pregnant
adj. embarazada, en cinta, en estado,
preñada *(vulgar)*
  to get pregnant
  quedar en estado
  to make (Elise) pregnant
  dejar (a Eliza) en estado, dejar
  (a Eliza) embarazada
priapic
adj. priápico (/-a)
priapism
n. el priapismo
prick
n. see "cock"
[private parts / privates]
n. las "partes"
promiscuity
n. la promiscuidad

promiscuous
adj. promiscuo (/-a)
prostate
n. la próstata
prostitute
n. la prostituta, la puta *(female)*;
el gigolo, el chulo *(male)*
   prostitute bar
   el bar de prostitutas, el puticlub
prostitution
n. la prostitución
provocative
adj. provocativo (/-a)
prude
n. [el mojigato / la mojigata],
[el pacato / la pacata]
prudish
adj. mojigato (/-a), pacato (/-a)
puberty
n. la pubertad
pubescent
adj. púber (/-a)
pubic hair
n. el vello púbico, el pendejo *(L.A.) (a
single hair)*; la pelambre, la pelambrera,
los pendejos *(L.A.) ("bush")*
punish
v. castigar
punishment
n. el castigo
pussy
n. el chocho *(see also "cunt")*
   pussy juice
   el flujo, el jugo del chocho
   pussy lips
   los labios del chocho

pussy-whipped, to be *(male)*
v. ser un calzonazos
quickie
n. el polvo rápido, el polvete, el qüickie
   to have a quickie
   echar un polvo rápido
rag, be on the
v. tener la regla
rape
n. la violación
v. violar
   date rape
   la violación por el chico con quien
   sales *(no exact equiv.)*
   gang rape
   n. la violación colectiva
   v. violar en grupo
rapist
n. el violador
raunch
n. las guarradas
raunchy
adj. guarro (/-a), obsceno (/-a)
rear end
n. el trasero, el culo
rectum
n. el recto
red-light district
n. el barrio chino *("Chinese quarter")*
redhead
n. [el pelirrojo / la pelirroja]
reject
v. rechazar, dar calabazas *("to give
pumpkins")*
relationship
n. la relación

meaningful relationship
la relación seria
monogamous relationship
la relación monógama
open relationship
la relación abierta
platonic relationship
la relación platónica
[remarry (Jim) / to get remarried (to Jim)]
v. volverse a casar (con Diego)
repressed
adj. reprimido (/-a), estrecho (/-a)
rod
n. la verga *(see also "cock")*
role-playing *(sexual)*
n. el disfrazarse
roll in the hay
n. el revolcón *(see also "lay")*
romance
n. el romance *(love affair),* lo romántico *(abstract concept)*
  summer romance
  el lío de verano
romantic
n. & adj. [(el) romántico / (la) romántica]
  hopeless romantic
  [el romántico perdido / la romántica perdida]
rope
n. la cuerda, la soga
rough
adv. a lo bruto, a lo duro
  rough fuck
  el polvo fuerte, la follada a lo bruto

rough sex
el sexo a lo bruto
to fuck rough
follar fuerte, follar a lo bruto
rub
v. frotar, dar un masaje
rubber
n. el condón, el preservativo, la goma
adj. de goma
rubdown
n. el masaje
S&M
n. el sadomasoquismo, el sadomaso, el S and M *(pron. as in Eng.)*
sadism
n. el sadismo
sadist
n. [el sádico / la sádica]
sadistic
adj. sádico (/-a)
sadomasochism
n. el sadomasoquismo
sadomasochist
n. [el / la] sadomasoquista, [el / la] sadomasoca
sadomasochistic
adj. sadomasoquista, sadomasoca
safe(r) sex
n. el sexo seguro
  unsafe sex
  el sexo peligroso
satyr
n. el sátiro
scat
n. la mierda *(shit),* la escatología *(as sex practice)*

scene
n. el ambiente
  the bar scene
  los bares, el mundillo de los bares
  S&M scene
  el ambiente sado-maso, el mundo
  del S and M
  singles scene
  el ambiente de solteros, el mundo de
  los solteros
score (with Fran)
v. tirarse, hacerse (a Paca)
screw
v. see "fuck"
scrotum
n. el escroto
seduce
v. seducir
seducer
n. [el seductor / la seductora]
seduction
n. la seducción
seductive
adj. seductor (/-a), seductivo (/-a)
seductress
n. la seductora
see-through
adj. transparente
  see-through blouse
  la blusa transparente
  see-through nightie
  el camisón transparente
selfish
adj. egoísta
semen
n. el semen, el esperma *(see also "[come / cum]")*

seminal fluid
n. el líquido seminal, el flujo (seminal)
sensitive
adj. sensible
[sensual / sensuous]
adj. sensual
sentimental
adj. sentimental
separated
adj. separado (/-a)
separation
n. la separación
  trial separation
  la separación provisional
sex
n. el sexo, el polvo, la follada,
el revolcón
  anonymous sex
  el sexo con [desconocidos /
  desconocidas]
  computer sex
  el sexo a través de ordenador *(Sp.)*,
  el sexo por computadora *(L.A.)*
  extramarital sex
  el sexo extramatrimonial
  group sex
  el sexo en grupo, la orgía
  hardcore sex
  el sexo a lo duro
  to have sex
  follar *(see also "fuck")*
  hot sex
  el sexo caliente, el sexo calentón
  kinky sex
  el sexo morboso, el sexo retorcido
  phone sex
  el sexo telefónico

premarital sex
el sexo prematrimonial
raunchy sex
el sexo guarro
rough sex
el sexo a lo bruto
safe(r) sex
el sexo seguro
sex appeal
el sex appeal, el atractivo
sex club
el sex-club, el club erótico, el antro
sex drive
el impulso (sexual), el empuje,
la libido
sex education
la educación sexual
sex [fiend / maniac]
el maníaco sexual
sex kitten
la gatita
sex life
la vida sexual
sex machine
la máquina de joder
sex partner
[el compañero / la compañera]
sexual
sex party
la orgía
sexpot *(female)*
el chocholoco
sex slave
[el esclavo / la esclava] sexual
sex-starved
hambriento (/-a), salido (/-a)

sex symbol
el sex-symbol, el ídolo *(masc. & fem.)*
sex therapy
la terapia sexual
sex toy
el juguete sexual
tender sex
el sexo suave, el sexo cariñoso
unsafe sex
el sexo peligroso
vanilla sex
el sexo tradicional
sexiness
n. el atractivo sexual
sexism
n. el sexismo
sexist
n. [el / la] sexista
sexologist
n. [el sexólogo / la sexóloga]
sexology
n. la sexología
sexual
adj. sexual
   sexual deviant
   [el desviado / la desviada] sexual
   sexual dysfunction
   el problema sexual
   sexual harassment
   el acoso sexual
   sexual intercourse
   las relaciones sexuales, el coito
   sexual organs
   los órganos sexuales, los genitales
   sexual orientation
   la orientación sexual

sexuality
n. la sexualidad
sexually-transmitted disease (STD)
n. la enfermedad de transmisión sexual (ETS)
sexy
adj. sexy
shack up (with)
v. vivir (con), vivir liado (/-a) (con)
   to be shacked up (with her)
   estar viviendo (con ella)
shame
n. la vergüenza, el pudor
shameless
adj. desvergonzado (/-a), sinvergüenza, descarado (/-a)
shape, in
adj. en forma
shapely *(female)*
adj. bien proporcionada, de buena figura
[shave / shave oneself]
v. [afeitar / afeitarse]
shaved
adj. afeitado (/-a)
   shaved legs
   las piernas afeitadas
   shaved pussy
   el chocho afeitado
shit
n. la mierda, la caca
v. cagar
short *(person)*
adj. bajo (/-a), pequeño (/-a)
shower
n. la ducha
v. ducharse

bridal shower
la despedida de soltera *("goodbye to the single woman")*
golden shower
la "lluvia dorada"
shrinking violet
n. la chica tímida *("shy girl")*
shy
adj. tímido (/-a)
shyness
n. la timidez
single
n. & adj. [(el) soltero / (la) soltera]
   singles bar
   el bar de ligue
   singles party
   la fiesta de solteros
   singles scene
   el ambiente de solteros
sixty-nine
n. el sesenta y nueve
v. hacer un sesenta y nueve
skin
n. la piel
   skin mag
   la revista porno
skirt chaser
n. el faldero
slap
n. la bofetada, el cachete
v. dar una bofetada, dar un cachete
slave
n. [el esclavo / la esclava]
   sex slave
   [el esclavo / la esclava] sexual
sleaze
n. [el vicioso / la viciosa], [el gamberro / la gamberra], [el guarro / la guarra]

to sleaze it up
gamberrear, hacer guarradas

sleaziness
n. el vicio, la guarrada

sleazy
adj. vicioso (/-a), gamberro (/-a), guarro (/-a)

sleep
v. dormir

to sleep around
ir de cama en cama, gamberrear, pendonear

to sleep together
dormir juntos

to sleep (with Roseanne)
dormir (con Rosana)

slim
adj. delgado (/-a)

slit *(of vagina)*
n. la raja

slut
n. la puta, el pendón *(see also "whore")*

smegma
n. el requesón

smooch
n. el beso
v. besuquear

smut
n. el porno, la pornografía

smutty
adj. porno, pornográfico (/-a)

snuggle (with)
v. acurrucarse, enroscarse (con)

social
adj. social

social life
la vida social

socialize (with James)
v. socializar, relacionarse (con Jaime)

sodomize
v. sodomizar

sodomy
n. la sodomía

softcore
adj. blando (/-a), de línea blanda

softcore mag
la revista de línea blanda

softcore porn
la pornografía blanda

sophisticate
n. [el sofisticado / la sofisticada]

sophisticated
adj. sofisticado (/-a)

spank
v. pegar (en el culo), azotar, dar nalgadas *(L.A.)*

spanking
n. la paliza (en el culo)

sperm
n. el esperma

spermicidal
adj. espermicida *(see also "contraceptive")*

spermicidal foam
la espuma espermicida

spermicidal jelly
la jalea espermicida

spermicide
n. el espermicida

spinster
n. la solterona

[spoon / sleep like spoons]
v. [estar / dormir] ajustados, [estar / dormir] encajados (en la cama)

spouse
n. [el esposo / la esposa]; [el / la] cónyuge

spread
v. abrir (de piernas) ("La abrí de piernas y la follé"—"I spread her legs and fucked her")

stacked
adj. tetona, pechugona

stag
adj. de soltero
  stag party
  la despedida de soltero *("farewell to the bachelor")*

stand up
v. dejar plantado (/-a) ("He stood me up"— "Me dejó plantada")

stiff
adj. tieso (/-a), duro (/-a)
  stiff cock
  la polla tiesa

stimulate
v. estimular

stimulating
adj. estimulante

stockings
n. las medias
  nylon stockings
  las medias de nylon
  lace stockings
  las medias de encaje
  silk stockings
  las medias de seda

stomach
n. el vientre, la barriga *(belly)*; el estómago *(organ)*

  on one's stomach
  boca abajo

straight
n. & adj. [(el) / (la)] heterosexual

strap
n. la correa, la tira

strings attached
adj. con condiciones
  no strings attached
  sin condiciones

strip
v. desnudarse
  striptease
  el striptease
  strip show
  el espectáculo de striptease

stripper
n. [la mujer / el hombre] que hace striptease *(no exact equiv.)*

strong
adj. fuerte

stud
n. el macho, el semental

studly
adj. macho, machote

stuff (it in)
v. meter(la) *(see also "fuck")*

submissive
adj. sumiso (/-a)

suck
v. chupar, mamar
  suck (off)
  chuparla, mamarla
  suck face
  besarse, morrear(se) ("We sucked face all night"—"Estuvimos morreando toda la noche")

sugar daddy
n. el protector, el caballo blanco ("*white horse*")

swallow
v. tragar

swap (partners)
v. intercambiar (parejas)

sweat
n. el sudor
v. sudar

sweaty
adj. sudoroso (/-a)

sweet
adj. dulce
  sweet nothings
  las tonterías, los susurros
  sweet talk
  las palabras dulces
  to sweet talk (Charlotte)
  convencer (a Carlota) con palabras dulces
  sweet young thing *(female)*
  la criatura encantadora

sweetheart (my)
n. (mi) cariño, (mi) corazón *(L.A.) (direct address)*; mi [novio / novia] *(referring to your sweetheart)*

swimsuit
n. el bañador, el traje de baño

swing
v. gamberrear, mariposear
  to swing both ways
  darle a los dos palos, irle los dos palos, jugar en los dos campos, ser bisexual ("*That guy swings both ways*"—"*A ese tipo le van los dos palos*")

swinger
n. [el gamberro / la gamberra]

swinging
adj. gamberro (/-a), de vida alegre
  to be a swinger
  irle la marcha ("*Paul's a swinger*"—"*A Pablo le va la marcha*")

syphilis
n. la sífilis

take (Emmanuelle) *(sexually)*
v. tomar (a Manuela)
  to take a leak
  hacer pis, echar un pis
  to take a shit
  cagar
  to take someone's cherry
  see "to deflower"

tall *(person)*
adj. alto (/-a)

tampon
n. el tampón

tan
n. el bronceado
v. broncearse, tomar el sol, ponerse moreno (/-a)

tanlines
n. las rayas del bañador

tanned
adj. bronceado (/-a), moreno (/-a)

tattoo
n. el tatuaje

tattooed
adj. tatuado (/-a)

tease *(sexual)*
n. la calientapollas
v. calentar la polla, mover el coño, mover el culo

teddy
n. el susana

tender
adj. tierno (/-a)

tenderness
n. la ternura

testicles
n. los testículos *(see also "balls")*

thigh
n. el muslo

thoughtful
adj. considerado (/-a)

thoughtless
adj. desconsiderado (/-a)

threeway
n. el trío, el ménage à trois
to have a threeway
montar(se) un trío, montar(se) un ménage à trois

throat
n. la garganta

tickle
v. hacer cosquillas

ticklish
adj. cosquilloso (/-a)

tie up
v. atar

tipsy
adj. alegre, achispado (/-a)

tit(s)
n. la(s) teta(s)

titclamp
n. la pinza para los pezones

titillate
v. excitar

titillating
adj. excitante

together
adv. juntos (/-as)

toilet
n. el wáter *(bowl)*; el baño, el lavabo *(bathroom)*

tongue
n. la lengua
v. lamer
tongue kiss
see "French kiss"

topless
adj. topless
to go topless
quedarse en topless
topless bar
el bar topless
topless beach
la playa topless

torch (for Tony), to carry a
v. sentir todavía algo (por Toño), alimentar el rescoldo (de Toño)

torso
n. el torso

torture
n. la tortura
v. torturar

touch
v. tocar
to touch oneself *(masturbate)*
tocarse, masturbarse

transsexual
n. & adj. [(el) / (la)] transexual

transvestite
n. [el travestido / la travestida], el travesti

trash it up *(sexually)*
v. gamberrear, putear

trick
n. el cliente (de prostituta)
  to turn tricks
  recibir clientes (la prostituta) *("the prostitute receiving customers")*

tryst
n. la cita

turned off
adj. sin ganas

turned on
adj. excitado (/-a), cachondo (/-a)

[turn-off / turn off]
n. algo que quita las ganas *(no exact equiv.;* "That's a real turn-off"—"Eso me quita las ganas")
v. quitar las ganas, cortar la leche ("He turns me off"—"Él me quita las ganas")

[turn-on / turn on]
n. algo que excita *(no exact equiv.;* "That's a turn-on"—"Eso me excita" or "Eso me pone caliente")
v. excitar, poner caliente, poner a cien ("You turn me on"—"Me pones a cien")

twat
n. see "cunt"

two-faced
adj. hipócrita

two-time
v. engañar, poner los cuernos ("You're two-timing me with Jane"—"Me estás engañando con Juanita")

two-timer
n. [el / la] infiel

two-timing
adj. infiel

ugly
n. feo (/-a)

unattractive
adj. no atractivo (/-a)

[uncircumcised / uncut] *(penis)*
adj. no circuncidado (/-a)

underage
adj. menor de edad

underwear
n. la ropa interior; el slip *(men)*; las bragas *(women)*

undress
v. desnudarse, desvestirse
  to undress (Frederick)
  desnudar a (Federico)

unfaithful
adj. infiel
  to be unfaithful (to Gus)
  ser infiel, poner los cuernos (a Gustavo)

unfeeling
adj. insensible

uninhibited
adj. desinhibido (/-a)

unmarried
adj. soltero (/-a)

untie
v. desatar

urinate
v. orinar

urine
n. la orina

vagina
n. la vagina

vaginal
adj. vaginal

Valentine's Day
n. el día de los enamorados, el día de San Valentín

vamp
n. la vampiresa
[venereal disease / VD]
n. la enfermedad venérea
vibrator
n. el vibrador
vice
n. el vicio
video
n. el vídeo
  porn video
  el vídeo porno
virgin
adj. virgen *(only as adj. to avoid refer-ring to the Virgin Mary; "I'm a virgin"—"Soy virgen")*
virginity
n. la virginidad
virile
adj. viril
virility
n. la virilidad
voluptuous
adj. voluptuosa
voyeur
n. [el / la] voyeur, el mirón *(male only)*
voyeuristic
adj. voyeur, mirón (/-a)
vulgar
adj. vulgar
vulva
n. la vulva
wallflower
n. la chica tímida *("shy girl")*
wank
n. & v. see "handjob" and "beat off"

want
v. querer *(romantically)*; desear *(sexually)*
wanton
adj. libertino (/-a), desenfrenado (/-a)
wasted *(on alcohol)*
adj. superborracho (/-a), superbebido (/-a), hecho (/-a) polvo, pasado (/-a)
  to get wasted
  emborracharse, pasarse [de alcohol / de drogas], mamarse
water-soluble
adj. hidrosoluble
water sports
n. la "lluvia dorada"
wedding
n. la boda, el matrimonio
church wedding
  la boda en la iglesia
  civil wedding
  la boda civil
  shotgun wedding
  la boda de penálty
  wedding anniversary
  el aniversario de bodas
  wedding ceremony
  la ceremonia matrimonial
  wedding ring
  el anillo matrimonial
well-built *(male)*
adj. macizo, cachas *(Sp.)*
well-hung
adj. bien dotado
well-preserved
adj. bien conservado (/-a)
wet
adj. mojado (/-a), húmedo (/-a)

wet cunt
el chocho húmedo, el chocho mojado

wet dream
el sueño húmedo

to have a wet dream
tener un sueño húmedo, correrse durmiendo

whack off
v. see "beat off"

"wham, bam, thank you, ma'am"
phr. picar y volar

whip
n. el látigo
v. pegar, azotar

whore
n. la puta

to act like a whore
ser muy puta, ser más puta que las gallinas *("to be sluttier than hens")*

to go whoring
ir de putas

guy who goes to whores
el putero

to whore around
ir de cama en cama

whorehouse
la casa de putas, el burdel, el puticlub

[widow / widower]
n. [la viuda / el viudo]

wife
n. la mujer, la esposa

trophy wife
la esposa vistosa

wife-swapping
el intercambio de parejas, el swinging

woman
n. la mujer

easy woman
la facilona, la fácil

kept woman
la mantenida

older woman
la mujer mayor, la mujer madura

"Women!"
"¡Faldas!" *("Skirts!")*

womanhood
n. la feminidad *(femininity)*

womanizer
n. el faldero, el mujeriego

womanly
adj. femenina

X-rated
adj. porno, pornográfico *(/-a)*

X-rated movie
la película porno

yeast infection
n. los hongos *("mushrooms")*

young
adj. joven

young girl
la joven

[young guy / man] *or* **youth**
el joven

young lady
la joven, la señorita

sweet young thing *(female)*
la criatura encantadora

youthful
adj. juvenil

zaftig *(female)*
adj. rolliza, llenita, rechoncha